# THE
# MOST
# HIGH
# GOD

# THE
# MOST
# HIGH
# GOD

## A Commentary
## On The Book Of Daniel

by

Renald E. Showers

# THE MOST HIGH GOD

Renald E. Showers

Copyright © 1982 by The Friends of Israel Gospel Ministry, Inc.
Bellmawr, NJ 08099

**Eleventh Printing** ................................2002

Library of Congress Catalog Card Number: 82-090990
ISBN 0-915540-30-4

Cover by Design Point, Inc., Salem, OR.

Visit our Web site at *www.foi.org*

# DEDICATION

*This book is dedicated to
Mr. and Mrs. John J. Frick
whose friendship and assistance
aided greatly in my
preparation for the ministry.*

# TABLE OF CONTENTS

# INTRODUCTION

## THE URGENCY OF THE TIME

This is a time of humanism, instability, war and false prophets and Christs. The rejection of God's rule which started for man in the Garden of Eden seems to be reaching a frenzied pitch. Man is determined to prove that he can rule the world in an orderly, meaningful way without God. He asserts that the ultimate purpose of everything is the glory and exaltation of man. His man-centered mania not only makes him refuse to submit to the rule of God but also renders him incapable of submitting (Rom. 8:7).

Because man rejects the rule of God, his pride drives him to do things opposite to what God has ordained. God ordained capital punishment for murderers, but man tries to abolish it. God regards human life as being valuable because He created it in His image, but man destroys it by the millions through abortion. God instituted marriage and ordained that it be permanent, but man divorces and suggests that marriage be abolished. God demands justice in society with the protection of the innocent and the punishment of the criminal, but man pampers the criminal at the expense of the innocent. God ordained the family as the nurturing place of future generations, but man proposes that government replace the family. God declares that the fear of the Lord is the starting point of wisdom, but man forbids any reference to God in the classroom. God instituted moral absolutes to govern man, but man says that Utopia can come only through the rejection of those absolutes. God ordained distinctive appearances and roles for the sexes, but man tries to obliterate those distinctions. God instituted sex to be used within the bonds of male-female marriage, but man perverts sex through pornography, fornication, adultery and homosexuality. God made man to have true meaning and purpose of life only in Him, but man tries to find true meaning in drugs, alcohol, the occult, materialism, philosophy, astrology, cults, transcendental meditation, fame and power.

Man has his false prophets and Christs to encourage him in his rebellious attempt at self-rule. These deceivers tell man that he is good and perfectible by nature. They teach that through the process of evolution man is moving toward divinity. Some so-called theologians declare that in order to have Utopia man must acclaim himself the great humanity divine. Others state that the true gospel is the good news that man is deified. Having willfully rejected the truth about God, man is worshiping and serving himself rather than his Creator.

Ironically, the more man tries to establish Utopia through self-rule the more his situation worsens. Instead of ruling the world in an orderly, meaningful way, he brings disorder, instability and chaos. Man pollutes his environment. His world is shaken by wars and threats of war. His streets are filled with violence and crime. His economy becomes uncontrollable. He is gripped with the fear of total annihilation by his own doomsday weapons. He bruises the very institutions which have given society stability, order and direction. He is haunted by the prospect of death and the fear that life has no ultimate purpose or meaning.

Man reels from one crisis to another. The more he insists

on going his own way, the more he batters and bloodies himself. However, instead of admitting that his rebellion against God is the cause of his problem, man stubbornly stands unbowed before the Lord of the universe. The more intense his predicament, the more entrenched is man's determination to prove that he can rule the world without God. Such firm resolve together with the worsening world situation makes man susceptible to the claims of an ultimate man — a man who opposes God, who seems to have the ability necessary to solve the world's problems and to rule the world well without God, a man who claims to have attained deity and has supernatural powers which appear to support that claim, a man who eventually demands total devotion from the human race and is the ultimate expression of absolute dictatorship and ruthless self-rule.

Man is enslaved already by his man-centered mania, but his acceptance of the claims and rule of an ultimate man will trap him in the pinnacle of slavery. Ironically, man's greatest effort to rid himself of the rule of God will not produce the freedom that he desires. Instead it will enslave him in the most fiendish, oppressive form of bondage. Rather than moving toward Utopia, man is hurtling toward the most horrible time of tribulation in world history. In light of the worsening world situation and man's growing susceptibility to the slavery of an ultimate man, there is an urgency about the present time. Man desperately needs to change his course by recognizing the root of his predicament — his rejection of the rule of God in favor of self-rule. If there were ever a time when man needed to be confronted with the sovereign rule of God and the serious consequences of rejecting that rule, the time is now.

## THE TIMELINESS OF THE BOOK OF DANIEL

In light of the present situation, no other book has a more

timely message for man than the biblical Book of Daniel. The theme of the book is the sovereign rule of God over the realm of man. Through events and prophecies recorded by Daniel, God demonstrates that He is sovereign over the Gentiles and Israel. His dealings with the Gentiles reveal that God rules over their kingdoms, punishments, rulers, defenses, law and future. His dealings with Israel manifest His sovereignty over its persecutions, preservation, salvation and final deliverance.

The key verse of the book emphasizes the sovereign rule of God: ". . . in order that the living may know that the Most High is ruler over the realm of mankind . . ." (4:17b).

Daniel charts the course that Gentile world dominion follows through history. It thereby deals with man's major attempts to rule the world apart from God through kingdom building. The book strips man's rule of its outward show of glory and exposes its inner beastly character. It shows how man's mania for self-rule drives one kingdom to devour another and compels the Gentiles to attempt the annihilation of God's special covenant people, Israel. Daniel foretells the grim climax of man's self-rule — Gentile world dominion will be dominated by an ultimate man who will oppose God, attempt to establish a one-world government, claim deity for himself and be the pinnacle of cruel dictators.

The Book of Daniel prophesies God's severe judgment of the ultimate man and man's self-rule in the future. It also tells how God will restore His full sovereign rule to the earth through His Messiah. Man's kingdoms of self-rule will be replaced by a literal, earthly Kingdom of God. Utopia will come, not by man's rule apart from God, but by man's submission to the rule of God which he rejected in Eden.

## THE BACKGROUND OF THE BOOK OF DANIEL

The Book of Daniel was written during the sixth century

(500's) B.C. It was a time of human pride, false religions, great Gentile kingdoms, war and the oppression of Israel.

The human author of the book was the prophet Daniel. Although some have tried to deny this authorship, no less a person than Jesus Christ has verified it. In Matthew 24:15 Jesus said: "Therefore when you see the ABOMINATION OF DESOLATION which was spoken of through Daniel the prophet. . . ." In light of this testimony, to deny that Daniel wrote the Book of Daniel is to deny the trustworthiness of Jesus Christ.

Daniel wrote his book while living in the royal courts of the city of Babylon. Thus, Babylon was the place of writing.

The Book of Daniel contains one of the most unique prophecies in all the Bible. With precision it foretold almost six centuries beforehand the exact time that Messiah would officially present Himself as Prince to Israel (9:25).

## A NOTE OF EXPLANATION

All quotations of the biblical text, unless otherwise noted, will be taken from the New American Standard Bible.

# THE HISTORICAL INTRODUCTION

## Chapter 1

# 1

## JEWISH YOUTHS
## IN A PAGAN CULTURE

### NEBUCHADNEZZAR'S FIRST
### EXPEDITION TO JERUSALEM (1:1-2)

*In the third year of the reign of Jehoiakim king of Judah,
Nebuchadnezzar king of Babylon came to Jerusalem and
besieged it. And the Lord gave Jehoiakim king of Judah into his
hand, along with some of the vessels of the house of God; and he
brought them to the land of Shinar, to the house of his god, and
he brought the vessels into the treasury of his god.*

The drums of war were beating in the Middle East. Egypt
and Babylon, the two superpowers of the late seventh
century B.C., were competing with each other for control of
that part of the world. It was only a matter of time before
these two powers would clash in a decisive battle. That
battle came in early summer of 605 B.C. when the
Babylonian army, under the leadership of Nebuchadnezzar,
the crown prince, attacked the Egyptian army at
Carchemish on the upper Euphrates River. The
Babylonians soundly defeated the Egyptians.[1] The Egyptians were forced to retreat south to their homeland. This
opened Palestine to the control of the Babylonians. As a
result, by August of 605 B.C. Nebuchadnezzar took
control of the city of Jerusalem.[2]

On August 15 or 16 Nebuchadnezzar's father, King
Nabopolassar, died in Babylon.[3] Nebuchadnezzar rushed
home to claim the throne. He was crowned king of Babylon
on the day of his arrival, September 6 or 7, 605 B.C.[4] On
this trip home, Nebuchadnezzar carried captive with him

some of the sacred vessels of the Temple of Jehovah in Jerusalem and the cream of the Jewish young men. Daniel and his companions were among those captives.

Nebuchadnezzar placed the vessels of Jehovah in Esagila, the temple of Marduk, the chief Babylonian god.[5] The king probably did this for two reasons. First, he wanted to express his gratitude to his god for the victories that had been granted to him. Thus, Nebuchadnezzar used the vessels of Jehovah as a thank offering to Marduk. Second, he wanted to exalt Marduk and humiliate Jehovah by asserting that Israel's God was subject to his god. To the pagan way of thinking, no nation could conquer another unless its god were more powerful than the god of the other. This action by Nebuchadnezzar would afford Jehovah a splendid opportunity to demonstrate two things. First, Jehovah isn't subject to any gods. He is the Most High, the Sovereign One of the universe. Second, it was Jehovah, not Marduk, who gave Nebuchadnezzar his victories. (Note: verse 2 clearly states that it was the Lord who gave the king of Judah and the sacred vessels of Jehovah into the hand of Nebuchadnezzar. God sovereignly did this to afford opportunity for a greater display of His sovereignty.)

## DANIEL AND HIS THREE JEWISH COMPANIONS (1:3-7)

*Then the king ordered Ashpenaz, the chief of his officials, to bring in some of the sons of Israel, including some of the royal family and of the nobles, youths in whom was no defect, who were good looking, showing intelligence in every branch of wisdom, endowed with understanding, and discerning knowledge, and who had ability for serving in the king's court; and he ordered him to teach them the literature and language of the Chaldeans. And the king appointed for them a daily ration from the king's choice food and from the wine which he drank, and appointed that they should be educated three years, at the end of which they were to enter the king's personal service. Now among them from the sons of Judah were Daniel, Hananiah, Mishael and Azariah. Then the commander of the officials assigned new names to them; and to Daniel he assigned the name Belteshazzar, to Hananiah Shadrach, to Mishael Meshach, and to Azariah Abed-nego.*

After Nebuchadnezzar became king, he commanded the chief marshall of his royal court to bring the best of the Jewish captives into the royal training school. Among these were young men from the royal family and nobility of Judah. This action fulfilled an earlier prophecy of God to the effect that offspring of the royal family of Judah would be taken captive to Babylon where they would become officials in the palace of the king of Babylon (Isa. 39:7).

The Jewish youths were fifteen to twenty years of age.[6] They were in excellent physical condition, handsome in appearance and keen intellectually. They were to be taught the writings and language of the Chaldeans. The Chaldeans were the elite, privileged class of several classes of wise men in Babylon. The kings of Babylon belonged to this class.[7] Thus, they were the most influential men of the kingdom and would have written extensively on many subjects. The Jewish youths probably were taught astronomy, astrology, mathematics, natural history, mythology, agriculture, architecture and the old languages of Babylon.[8] They were given the best education that Babylon afforded. The training lasted for three years. It was designed to prepare the young men to become officers in the king's service.

It was an oriental custom to feed officers of the royal court the choice food and wine from the king's table.[9] Inasmuch as the young men were training to become officers, Nebuchadnezzar commanded that this privilege be extended to them as well.

Among the Jewish trainees were four young men whose Hebrew names honored Jehovah, the God of Israel. The name Daniel meant *God is judge.* Hananiah signified

*Jehovah is gracious.* Mishael expressed the question, *who is
what God is?* Azariah conveyed the meaning, *Jehovah has
helped.*[10] It wasn't long before an official assigned them
Babylonian names that honored Babylonian gods. Daniel
was assigned Belteshazzar *(Bel protect his life)* after a chief
Babylonian god, Bel. Hananiah was given Shadrach
*(command of Aku)* after the moon-god, Aku. Mishael was
designated Meshach *(who is what Aku is?).* Azariah was
named Abed-nego *(servant of Nebo)* after the god Nebo
(nego was a corrupted spelling of Nebo).[11] This change of
names probably was intended to bring a mind set change in
the Jewish youths. No longer were they to think like Jews
and be loyal to Jehovah. Now they were to think like
Babylonians and be loyal to the Babylonian gods.

The pressure to conform to Babylon's pagan culture was
severe upon Daniel and his friends. They belonged to a
conquered, humiliated people. They had been uprooted
from families, friends, familiar surroundings — from
everything that had given them security and meaning in life.
They had been transported hundreds of miles to a totally
strange environment to live among total strangers. In this
new setting they were a small minority. They were only teen-
agers subjected to the authority of the most powerful adult
ruler on earth. It appeared that their God had been
humiliated. They were put under the instruction of elite but
ungodly teachers, men who were regarded as the world's top
scholars — a situation that could be deadly for the faith of
impressionable teens. Their education exposed them to such
anti-God subjects as astrology and pagan mythology. They
were placed in the enviable position of gaining favorable
government posts, if they would cooperate fully with their
rulers. They were afforded what many would have regarded
as a great privilege — the eating of the king's fare. With the
change of names, one of the major things that had given
them personal identity since birth was removed. Was their

commitment to Jehovah strong enough to withstand this onslaught of pressure? One aspect of the pressure provided the specific test that would tell — namely, the giving of the king's food to the students.

Eating the fare of a Gentile king posed a twofold problem for a Jew faithful to Jehovah. First, it contained food that God in the Mosaic Law had forbidden the Jews to eat. Second, the king's food was offered as a sacrifice to the Babylonian gods before it was eaten.[12] To the Babylonian way of thinking, to eat that food was to participate in the worship of their gods. Thus, if a Jew were to eat the king's fare, he would appear to have forsaken Jehovah for the worship of idols.

## THE ABSTENTION OF DANIEL AND HIS FRIENDS (1:8-16)

*But Daniel made up his mind that he would not defile himself with the king's choice food or with the wine which he drank; so he sought permission from the commander of the officials that he might not defile himself. Now God granted Daniel favor and compassion in the sight of the commander of the officials, and the commander of the officials said to Daniel, "I am afraid of my lord the king, who has appointed your food and your drink; for why should he see your faces looking more haggard than the youths who are your own age? Then you would make me forfeit my head to the king." But Daniel said to the overseer whom the commander of the officials had appointed over Daniel, Hananiah, Mishael and Azariah, "Please test your servants for ten days, and let us be given some vegetables to eat and water to drink. Then let our appearance be observed in your presence, and the appearance of the youths who are eating the king's choice food; and deal with your servants according to what you see." So he listened to them in this matter and tested them for ten days. And at the end of ten days their appearance seemed better and they were fatter than all the youths who had been eating the king's choice food. So the overseer continued to withhold their choice food and the wine they were to drink, and kept giving them vegetables.*

The four Jewish youths were faced with a dilemma. If they ate the king's food, they would stir up the wrath of God; if they did not eat, they would be in serious trouble with their captors. They could have tried to rationalize their way around obedience to Jehovah. They could have said: "Under normal circumstances God's Law is to be obeyed, but we are in an abnormal circumstance. Surely God doesn't expect total obedience to every precept of His Law in such a unique situation as ours." They might have asserted: "God is to blame for this. If He had not put us in this awful predicament, it would not have been necessary for us to break His Law." They could have reasoned: "If we eat the king's food, we shall be placed in government posts. Think of the great impact we can have for Jehovah by being in such influential positions. Certainly God must regard this opportunity to serve Him in such a big way as being more important than obedience to His Law." Again, they could have said: "If we disobey the king, it may cost us our lives. Surely in God's value system the preservation of human life is of greater consequence than obedience to Him." Finally, they could have contended: "If we refuse to eat the king's food, it may cost the life of the official who is responsible to see that we eat. Would not love dictate that we eat the food in order to preserve the official's life? Does not love overrule obedience to a divine command?"

Thankfully, the four youths did not resort to such false rationalizations. Daniel determined not to defile himself with the king's fare. It would appear that his three friends did the same. When Daniel decided to obey God, he did not go on a fanatical rampage that would have reflected negatively on Jehovah. Instead, he went through proper channels. He approached the chief marshall and requested permission to abstain from the king's fare. He honestly explained the reason for his request.

God sovereignly prompted the chief marshall to respect

Daniel's request. He wanted to grant it but could not, for to do so might cost him his head. He feared that if the four Jewish youths abstained from the king's fare, they would appear more unhealthy than the other students when it was time to be examined by the king.

Having learned that the major concern of the chief marshall was the appearance of the youths, Daniel approached their immediate supervisor with the following request: "For ten days give my three friends and me vegetables and water instead of the king's fare. Then compare us with the youths who eat the king's fare to see which are more healthy in appearance. After this test, deal with us accordingly." This was a step of faith for Daniel and his friends. They were trusting God to honor their obedience to Him.

God sovereignly honored their stand. He moved their supervisor to grant the test. At the end of the ten days the four Jewish youths were more healthy in appearance than the others. As a result, they were excused from the requirement of eating the king's fare.

## THE PROGRESS OF THE FOUR JEWISH YOUTHS AND THEIR ENTRANCE INTO THE KING'S SERVICE (1:17-21)

*And as for these four youths, God gave them knowledge and intelligence in every branch of literature and wisdom; Daniel even understood all kinds of visions and dreams. Then at the end of the days which the king had specified for presenting them, the commander of the officials presented them before Nebuchadnezzar. And the king talked with them, and out of them all not one was found like Daniel, Hananiah, Mishael and Azariah; so they entered the king's personal service. And as for every matter of wisdom and understanding about which the king consulted them, he found them ten times better than all the magicians and conjurers who were in all his realm. And Daniel continued until the first year of Cyrus the King.*

God enabled Daniel and his friends to learn their subjects well. He gave them a gift of wisdom so that they could distinguish true knowledge from the false. To Daniel He gave the added gift of discerning between true and false dreams and visions and of interpreting the true ones accurately. These abilities were crucial for a follower of Jehovah living in a land that stressed visions and dreams.

After the three years of education all the young trainees were tested before King Nebuchadnezzar. Daniel and his three friends so far surpassed the others in their performance that they were placed in the king's service. They even surpassed by ten times all the king's experienced magicians and enchanters. This was due, not to natural ability on their part, but to God's special enablement.

In spite of the fact that they had obeyed God instead of the king, Daniel and his friends were advanced to government posts. The sovereignty of God was sufficient to get them there without their resorting to faulty rationalizations around obedience to His command. Through this experience they had demonstrated that a saint of God is to obey Him no matter what the circumstances and to let the results rest in His sovereign hands.

Verse 21 declares that Daniel continued until the first year of Cyrus, the King of Medo-Persia. This is not a contradiction of chapter ten, verse one, which talks about Daniel receiving a message in the third year of Cyrus. Verse 21 does not say that Daniel died in the first year of Cyrus. The verse is simply a summary statement which ends the historical introduction of the book. The first year of Cyrus was the end of Babylon's rule. Thus, the verse is saying that Daniel survived the entire Babylonian rule in spite of all the oriental intrigue of that rule. This again is a testimony to God's sovereignty.

# GOD'S SOVEREIGN RULE IN THE KINGDOM OF MEN DEMONSTRATED

## Chapters 2-12

# PART I:

## GOD'S SOVEREIGN RULE OVER GENTILES DEMONSTRATED

### Chapters 2-7

# 2

# GOD'S RULE OVER GENTILE EMPIRES DEMONSTRATED

## A NOTE OF EXPLANATION

Chapters 2:4b-7:28 of the Book of Daniel were written in the Aramaic language, whereas the rest of the book was written in the Hebrew language. Why would Daniel, who was a Hebrew, write a major portion of his book in the Aramaic language? During and after Daniel's time, Aramaic was an international language. It was the common diplomatic and business language of the nations, understood by Gentiles and Jews. Since chapters 2-7 of Daniel deal with Jehovah's rule over the Gentiles, Daniel wrote those chapters in the language that Gentiles could understand. Had he written them in Hebrew, their message would have been missed by most Gentiles of that time.[1]

## NEBUCHADNEZZAR'S DREAM AND THE FAILURE OF HIS WISE MEN (2:1-13)

*Now in the second year of the reign of Nebuchadnezzar, Nebuchadnezzar had dreams; and his spirit was troubled and his sleep left him. Then the king gave orders to call in the magicians, the conjurers, the sorcerers and the Chaldeans, to tell the king his dreams. So they came in and stood before the king. And the king said to them, "I had a dream, and my spirit is anxious to understand the dream." Then the Chaldeans spoke to the king in Aramaic: "O king, live forever! Tell the dream to your servants, and we will declare the interpretation." The king answered and said to the Chaldeans, "The command from me is firm: if you do not make known to me the dream and its interpretation, you will be torn limb from limb, and your houses will be made a rubbish*

*heap. But if you declare the dream and its interpretation, you
will receive from me gifts and a reward and great honor;
therefore, declare to me the dream and its interpretation." They
answered a second time and said, "Let the king tell the dream to
his servants, and we will declare the interpretation." The king
answered and said, "I know for certain that you are bargaining
for time, inasmuch as you have seen that the command from me
is firm, that if you do not make the dream known to me, there is
only one decree for you. For you have agreed together to speak
lying and corrupt words before me until the situation is changed;
therefore tell me the dream, that I may know that you can
declare to me its interpretation." The Chaldeans answered the
king and said, "There is not a man on earth who could declare
the matter for the king, inasmuch as no great king or ruler has
ever asked anything like this of any magician, conjurer or
Chaldean. Moreover, the thing which the king demands is
difficult, and there is no one else who could declare it to the king
except gods, whose dwelling place is not with mortal flesh."
Because of this the king became indignant and very furious, and
gave orders to destroy all the wise men of Babylon. So the decree
went forth that the wise men should be slain; and they looked for
Daniel and his friends to kill them.*

In 603 B.C. Nebuchadnezzar had a dream that disturbed
him so much that he could not continue to sleep.[2] He called
in all classes of his wise men to deal with his dream. Up to
this point the wise men had had an easy job with regard to
royal dreams. They could give any interpretation that
sounded reasonable, once the king had related the content
of the dream. Therefore, they asked the king to relate the
dream. This time, however, Nebuchadnezzar decided to test
his wise men. He demanded that they not only interpret the
dream but also tell him its content. The king commanded
severe judgment if they failed.[3] Their bodies were to be torn
apart limb from limb, and their houses were to be made into
public restrooms (cf. 2 Ki. 10:27).[4] On the other hand, the
wise men were to be rewarded greatly if they met the king's
demand.

The wise men knew that they could not fulfill the king's
demand. In order to postpone their impending deaths, they

pretended that they had not heard the king's requirement. They asked him a  second time to relate the dream. Nebuchadnezzar, recognizing their delay tactic, became more emphatic in his demand. The elite Chaldeans told the king that he was unreasonable — no great ruler had ever made such a demand. He was requiring something that was humanly impossible — only the gods could do what he wanted. These insults from the very class of wise men to which the king himself belonged were more than Nebuchadnezzar could tolerate. In a fit of rage he ordered all the wise men of Babylon to be killed. Although Daniel and his friends were not present in this session, they were to be executed too. Once again God was presented with a fine opportunity to intervene and display His sovereignty.

## DANIEL'S REQUESTS; GOD'S ANSWER; DANIEL'S THANKSGIVING PRAYER (2:14-24)

*Then Daniel replied with discretion and discernment to Arioch, the captain of the king's bodyguard, who had gone forth to slay the wise men of Babylon; he answered and said to Arioch, the king's commander, "For what reason is the decree from the king so urgent?" Then Arioch informed Daniel about the matter. So Daniel went in and requested of the king that he would give him time, in order that he might declare the interpretation to the king. Then Daniel went to his house and informed his friends, Hananiah, Mishael and Azariah, about the matter, in order that they might request compassion from the God of heaven concerning this mystery, so that Daniel and his friends might not be destroyed with the rest of the wise men of Babylon. Then the mystery was revealed to Daniel in a night vision. Then Daniel blessed the God of heaven; Daniel answered and said, "Let the name of God be blessed forever and ever, for wisdom and power belong to Him. And it is He who changes the times and the epochs; He removes kings and establishes kings; He gives wisdom to wise men, and knowledge to men of understanding. It is He who reveals the profound and hidden things; He knows what is in the darkness, and the light dwells with him. To Thee,*

*O God of my fathers, I give thanks and praise, for Thou hast given me wisdom and power; even now Thou hast made known to me what we requested of Thee, for Thou hast made known to us the king's matter." Therefore Daniel went in to Arioch, whom the king had appointed to destroy the wise men of Babylon; he went and spoke to him as follows: "Do not destroy the wise men of Babylon! Take me into the king's presence, and I will declare the interpretation to the king."*

When Daniel heard about the king's order against the wise men, he requested that the king grant him a certain amount of time. Daniel promised in return to fulfill the king's demand by the end of that time. This was another step of faith. Daniel was trusting God to reveal the content and interpretation of the king's dream.

Having been granted the time requested, Daniel rushed home and reported the situation to his friends. Together they held an emergency prayer meeting. They petitioned Jehovah to reveal the necessary information to them. God answered their prayer by revealing the matter to Daniel. Daniel responded by uttering a great prayer of thanksgiving. In this prayer Daniel emphasized the wisdom, power and sovereignty of God.

Now that Daniel had the necessary information, he requested to be brought before the king to fulfill Nebuchadnezzar's demand. By the grace of Jehovah, the lives of the wise men would be spared.

## DANIEL'S APPEARANCE
## BEFORE THE KING (2:25-30)

*Then Arioch hurriedly brought Daniel into the king's presence and spoke to him as follows: "I have found a man among the exiles from Judah who can make the interpretation known to the king!" The king answered and said to Daniel, whose name was Belteshazzar, "Are you able to make known to me the dream which I have seen and its interpretation?" Daniel answered before the king and said, "As for the mystery about which the king has inquired, neither wise men, conjurers, magicians, nor diviners are able to declare it to the king. However, there is a God in heaven who reveals mysteries, and He has made known to King Nebuchadnezzar what will take place in the latter days. This was your dream and the visions in your mind while on your bed. As for you, O king, while on your bed your thoughts turned to what would take place in the future; and He who reveals mysteries has made known to you what will take place. But as for me, this mystery has not been revealed to me for any wisdom residing in me more than in any other living man, but for the purpose of making the interpretation known to the king, and that you may understand the thoughts of your mind.*

Daniel told Nebuchadnezzar very frankly that his demand was humanly impossible to fulfill. Only the God in heaven could do it. Daniel made it clear that it was that God who had given the king his dream. He also declared that the dream revealed what would happen in the future and the latter days. Daniel refused to take any credit to himself for fulfilling the king's demand. All the credit belonged to God.

## THE CONTENT OF THE DREAM (2:31-35)

*"You, O king, were looking and behold, there was a single great statue; that statue, which was large and of extraordinary splendor, was standing in front of you, and its appearance was awesome. The head of that statue was made of fine gold, its breast and its arms of silver, its belly and its thighs of bronze, its legs of iron, its feet partly of iron and partly of clay. You continued looking until a stone was cut out without hands, and it struck the statue on its feet of iron and clay, and crushed them. Then the iron, the clay, the bronze, the silver and the gold were crushed all at the same time, and became like chaff from the summer threshing floors; and the wind carried them away so that not a trace of them was found. But the stone that struck the statue became a great mountain and filled the whole earth.*

Daniel indicated that the dream consisted of an image and a stone. The image was human in form and was so huge and brilliant that it was terrifying to see. Its head was made of gold. Its breast and arms consisted of silver. Its belly and two thighs were composed of bronze. Its two legs were comprised of iron, and its feet and toes were a mixture of iron and clay.

The stone of the dream had been cut out of a mountain (cf. v. 45) without hands. This indicated that the stone was not human in origin. The stone struck the feet of the image with such force that the feet were crushed. This caused all the substances of the entire image to disintegrate into the consistency of chaff. The wind blew away every remnant of the image. Then the stone became a large mountain that filled the entire earth.

## THE INTERPRETATION
## OF THE DREAM (2:36-45)

*"This was the dream; now we shall tell its interpretation before the king. You, O king, are the king of kings, to whom the God of heaven has given the kingdom, the power, the strength, and the glory; and wherever the sons of men dwell, or the beasts of the field, or the birds of the sky, He has given them into your hand and has caused you to rule over them all. You are the head of gold. And after you there will arise another kingdom inferior to you, then another third kingdom of bronze, which will rule over all the earth. Then there will be a fourth kingdom as strong as iron; inasmuch as iron crushes and shatters all things, so, like iron that breaks in pieces, it will crush and break all these in pieces. And in that you saw the feet and toes, partly of potter's clay and partly of iron, it will be a divided kingdom; but it will have in it the toughness of iron, inasmuch as you saw the iron mixed with common clay. And as the toes of the feet were partly of iron and partly of pottery, so some of the kingdom will be strong and part of it will be brittle. And in that you saw the iron mixed with common clay, they will combine one with another in the seed of men; but they will not adhere to one another, even as iron does not combine with pottery. And in the days of those kings the God of heaven will set up a kingdom which will never be destroyed, and that kingdom will not be left for another*

*people; it will crush and put an end to all these kingdoms, but it will itself endure forever. Inasmuch as you saw that a stone was cut out of the mountain without hands and that it crushed the iron, the bronze, the clay, the silver, and the gold, the great God has made known to the king what will take place in the future; so the dream is true, and its interpretation is trustworthy."*

Daniel began the interpretation of the dream by asserting the sovereignty of God. He declared that it was the God of heaven, not the Babylonian gods nor the king himself, who had made Nebuchadnezzar the top ruler of the then-known world. It took courage for Daniel to speak this way to the king. The pressure would have been great to win the king's favor and to avoid statements that might be offensive. Daniel was determined, however, not to sacrifice the truth of God on the altar of expediency.

Daniel called Jehovah the God of heaven not just because heaven is God's special dwelling place. The Babylonians believed that their gods came from the earth.[5] Daniel wanted to make it clear that his God was not one of the Babylonian gods.

It is important to note that in the interpretation Daniel moved progressively from the top to the bottom of the image. This downward movement represented the passage of time. Thus, the upper parts of the image portrayed earlier history, and the lower parts portrayed later history.

When Daniel interpreted the head of gold, he said to Nebuchadnezzar: "You are the head of gold. And after you there will arise another kingdom inferior to you." Thus, the head of gold represented both the Babylonian kingdom and its great king.[6] Orientals regarded kings and their kingdoms as being synonymous with each other.

Why did God represent Babylon with gold in the dream? It was an appropriate representation for two reasons. First, Marduk, the chief god of Babylon, was called the god of gold.[7] Second, Babylon used gold extensively in its

buildings, images and shrines. Herodotus, who was at
Babylon ninety years after the era of Nebuchadnezzar, was
astonished at the amount of gold there. Even walls and
buildings were overlaid with gold.[8]

Babylon was to be succeeded by a second kingdom,
represented by the image's breast and arms of silver (v. 39).
This would be the kingdom of Medo-Persia. Two arms
coming together to form one breast pictured this kingdom
perfectly. Two distinct peoples, the Medes and the Persians,
were united together in 550 B.C. under the same king to
form one great power.[9]

Why was silver a fitting representation of the Medo-
Persian kingdom? In ancient times silver signified money,
for silver was the standard of value and the medium of
exchange. Medo-Persia became noted for basing its power
on money which was collected through an extensive tax
system (Ezra 4:13; Dan. 11:2).[10]

Daniel stated that Medo-Persia would be inferior to
Babylon. It was not inferior to Babylon in military strength,
for it conquered Babylon. It was not inferior in size, for
Medo-Persia was a much larger kingdom than Babylon. It
was inferior in one respect. Being a partnership empire, it
lacked the absolute unity that Babylon enjoyed.[11]

This prophecy of the dream was fulfilled when Medo-
Persia conquered Babylon in 539 B.C.[12]

Medo-Persia was to be succeeded by a third Gentile
kingdom represented by the image's belly and thighs of
bronze (v. 39). This would be the kingdom of Greece under
Alexander the Great and his successors. One belly sub-
divided into two thighs was an excellent way for God to
portray the Grecian kingdom ahead of time. After Alexander had unified his kingdom, he died at a young age. His
kingdom was divided among his four leading generals.
However, only two of the divisions played an important role
in history. Those two divisions headquartered in Syria and

Egypt.[13]

Why did God represent Greece with bronze? The Greeks developed this metal highly and used it extensively in their implements of war.[14] Thus, their kingdom was characterized by bronze.

Daniel said that Greece would rule over all the earth, referring to the world then known to Daniel and his contemporaries. It is a fact that Alexander's kingdom ruled considerably more of the earth than did Babylon and Medo-Persia.

This part of the prophetic dream was fulfilled when Greece conquered Persia in 331 B.C.[15]

Greece was to be succeeded by a fourth Gentile kingdom represented by the image's legs of iron and feet and toes of iron and clay (vv. 40-43). This would be the Roman Empire. God's portrayal of Rome with two legs was very apt, for the ancient Roman Empire ruled extensive areas of both the western and eastern divisions of the world. In fact, in 364 A.D. the Roman Empire was divided politically into two divisions — the Western Roman Empire with Rome as its capital and the Eastern Roman Empire with Constantinople as its capital.[16]

Iron was an excellent designation of Rome for at least two reasons. First, ancient Rome was noted for its use of iron in its military weaponry.[17] Second, as Daniel indicated in verse forty, just as iron is able to crush gold, silver and bronze because it is stronger, so Rome would crush and shatter the ancient world. Ancient Rome did just that through its great military strength.

This aspect of the prophetic dream was fulfilled when Rome conquered Greece by 146 B.C.[18]

As noted earlier, Daniel's downward movement on the image represented the passage of time. Thus, when Daniel interpreted the last part of the image — the feet and toes — he was dealing with the final form of Gentile world dominion in time. Since the feet and toes were part of the representation of the fourth or Roman kingdom, they portrayed the Roman Empire in its final stage of existence in contrast with its earlier leg stage.

The legs of the fourth kingdom consisted of iron, but the feet and toes were a mixture of iron and clay. This distinction in substance also indicated that the Roman Empire would experience two distinct stages of existence — an earlier and a later stage.

Daniel interpreted the iron and clay mixture as follows: just as iron is strong, so the final stage of the Roman Empire would be strong militarily. Just as clay is characterized by brittleness, so the final stage of the Roman Empire would be characterized by division. Different groups of people would combine with one another to form the final stage of the empire, but they would not adhere completely to one another, just as iron and clay do not combine completely with each other.

It would appear, then, that the final stage of the Roman Empire would consist of a confederation of several nations. These nations would combine forces for the sake of military strength, but they would not combine to the extent of losing their national identities and distinctives. Inasmuch as the image of the dream was human in form, it would have had ten toes. This indicated that the final stage of the Roman Empire would consist of a ten nation confederation. Indeed, Daniel 7:23-24 clearly stated that the fourth or Roman kingdom would consist eventually of ten kings or kingdoms (cf. Rev. 17:12).

As noted earlier, the iron legs represented the ancient Roman Empire as it devoured massive areas of the world through brute military strength. But when was the later foot and toe stage to exist? Inasmuch as the Roman Empire never consisted of a ten nation confederation in past history, one is forced to conclude that this final stage of Rome's existence must take place in the future.

Sometime beyond the present there will be a revival of the Roman Empire. The empire that died in 476 A.D. will be brought to life again in the form of a ten nation confederation. Many are convinced that the Common Market of Europe will develop into this empire. It is a fact that political leaders of several European nations have met within recent years to discuss the formation of such a confederation — a confederation which will be united for military and economic strength, but will maintain the identities and distinctives of the member nations. Western leaders are thinking in that direction.

Rome was to be succeeded by a fifth kingdom represented by the stone in the dream (vv. 44-45). This kingdom would be set up by the God of heaven, not by man. The characteristics of this Kingdom of God would be as follows: it would never be destroyed; no other kingdoms would ever succeed it; it would destroy and end all the Gentile kingdoms portrayed in the image of the dream; it would endure forever. These characteristics of God's kingdom would be a stark contrast with the characteristics of the Gentile kingdoms.

The Babylonians called their chief god, Marduk, "The Great Mountain."[19] They believed that their gods came from the sacred mountain of the earth — the mountain that they called "the Mountain of the Lands."[20] The temples of Babylon were intended to be imitations of mountains.[21] All of this indicates that to the Babylonian way of thinking, mountains were associated with what is divine. Because of this Babylonian mind set, God purposely portrayed His future kingdom first as a stone cut out of a mountain and second as a stone that becomes a great mountain (v. 35). This was His way of getting Nebuchadnezzar to understand that the fifth kingdom would be divine rather than human in origin. This kingdom would not be another attempt by man to rule the earth apart from God. God emphasized this divine origin by portraying the stone as cut out without human hands. But to prevent Nebuchadnezzar from concluding that this divine kingdom would be set up by Babylonian gods, Daniel made it clear that the God of heaven would establish it.

The stone struck the huge image on its feet, thereby causing the entire image to disintegrate. This indicated several things. First, the coming of the Kingdom of God would take place when the last stage of Rome — the Revived Roman Empire — would be in existence. Second, the Kingdom of God would destroy the Revived Roman Empire when it would come. Third, when the Kingdom of God would destroy the last stage of the Roman Empire, it thereby would destroy all of Gentile world dominion, for the Revived Roman Empire would be the last representative of that dominion.

After the stone had crushed the entire image, the wind blew away every remnant of it. The Babylonians believed that wind was a divine activity. They called Marduk "Lord of the Wind."[22] As a result of this belief, Nebuchadnezzar would understand that the divine activity would rid the earth of Gentile world power.

Once every remnant of the image had been removed from the earth, the stone became a great mountain and filled the whole earth (v. 35). The Babylonians pictured the earth as a great mountain. They called the earth "Mountain-house."[23] In light of this Babylonian concept, God portrayed His kingdom as a great mountain which filled the earth to make one thing clear — although the fifth kingdom would be set up by the God of heaven, it would be a kingdom on earth just as the four Gentile kingdoms had been. It would rule the earth of its day just as the Gentile kingdoms ruled the known earth of their days.

As noted earlier, the ancient Orient regarded kings and

kingdoms as being synonymous. In light of this, the stone of the dream must be a representation, not only of the Kingdom of God, but also of its King. Other prophetic portions of the Bible indicated that that King would be the person who is called the Messiah (Ps. 2:2), the Son of God (Ps. 2:4-12) and the Son of Man who comes with the clouds of heaven (Dan. 7:13-14). The Bible also indicated that Jesus Christ is that person (Mt. 16:16; 26:63-64). It can be concluded, then, that the stone represented both the Kingdom of God and Jesus Christ. Significantly, more than once the Bible referred to Jesus as the Stone (Mt. 21:33-45; 1 Pet. 2:4-8).

Since the stone represented both Jesus Christ and the Kingdom of God, its appearance in the dream portrayed the coming of Christ to establish that kingdom. The fact that the Bible presented two comings of Christ prompts an important question: would Christ establish the Kingdom of God during His first or second coming? Some have concluded that the divine kingdom of Daniel 2 was established by Christ during His first coming and that the kingdom is totally spiritual in nature. According to this view, the kingdom consists either of the Church or the spiritual rule of Christ in human hearts, and the Gentile kingdom which was crushed by the Kingdom of God was the ancient Roman Empire, not a future Revived Roman Empire.

This view has some problems. First, earlier observations indicated that Christ would come to establish the Kingdom of God when Rome would be in its foot and toe stage — the ten nation confederation stage. They also indicated that the confederation stage of the Roman Empire must yet be future, because the ancient empire never consisted of a ten nation confederation. Thus, one is forced to conclude that the coming of Christ which was portrayed by the appearance of the stone must be His future second coming.

Second, Daniel 2:44 stated that the Kingdom of God

would be set up "in the days of those kings." To what kings did Daniel refer? It would appear that Daniel had in mind the kings who would rule the ten nation Revived Roman Empire of the future. Again this would indicate that the Kingdom of God would come in conjunction with Christ's second coming.

Third, the imagery of the dream seemed to suggest no coexistence of the Roman Empire and the actual Kingdom of God. The appearance of the stone cut out without hands represented the coming of Christ to establish the kingdom. After the stone crushed the image, every remnant of the image was blown away before the stone became a great mountain and filled the earth (vv. 34-35). This indicated that every remnant of the Roman Empire would be gone before the actual Kingdom of God would be established to rule the earth. In contrast with this imagery, the view which concludes that the Kingdom of God was established during Christ's first coming would require several centuries of coexistence of the Roman Empire and the actual Kingdom of God. It is a fact of history that the Western Roman Empire lasted more than four hundred years after Christ's first coming. Indeed, the Eastern Roman Empire lasted more than fourteen hundred years after that coming.

Fourth, the imagery of the dream corresponds with John's description of Christ's second coming and Millennial rule. In Revelation 19 and 20, John indicated that, when Christ would appear in His second coming, He would crush Gentile world power, then would rule the earth for one thousand years. This Millennial rule would be only the first phase of the future Kingdom of God — the phase for this present earth. After the Millennium, the Kingdom of God would continue forever on the new eternal earth (Rev. 21-22).

For reasons such as these, it can be concluded that the dream of Daniel 2 indicated that the future Kingdom of God would be established in conjunction with the second coming of Christ. Since it would take the place of the four Gentile kingdoms, it would be a literal, earthly kingdom just as they.

Several final observations concerning the image of the dream should be made. First, the downward movement on the image not only represented the passage of time, but also revealed a descending decrease in value of the substances of the image.[24] The intended lesson seemed to be this: the longer man would attempt to rule the earth apart from God, the more degenerated that rule would become. Second, the downward movement on the image also revealed an ascending growth in strength of the substances.[25] The longer man would attempt to rule the earth apart from God, the more that rule would be characterized by militarism.

Third, God designed the image to portray the times when the Gentiles would be the dominant power in the world and the Jews would be at the mercy of that power. Jesus called those times "the times of the Gentiles" (Lk. 21:24). According to the dream, those times began with Babylon in the late 600's B.C. and would continue until the second coming of Christ.

The ultimate purpose of Nebuchadnezzar's dream was to assert the sovereign rule of God in the affairs of men and His superiority over the pagan gods. Not only did it show the future course of Gentile world dominion, but also the destruction of that dominion by God and the replacement of it with His kingdom that would last forever. Since the pagans thought that no kingdom could conquer another kingdom unless its god were more powerful than the god of the other, the fact that the Kingdom of the God of heaven would conquer all of Gentile world dominion would indicate the superiority of the God of heaven to all the Gentile gods.

# NEBUCHADNEZZAR'S RESPONSE (2:46-49)

*Then King Nebuchadnezzar fell on his face and did homage to Daniel, and gave orders to present to him an offering and fragrant incense. The king answered Daniel and said, "Surely your God is a God of gods and a Lord of kings and a revealer of mysteries, since you have been able to reveal this mystery." Then the king promoted Daniel and gave him many great gifts, and he made him ruler over the whole province of Babylon and chief prefect over all the wise men of Babylon. And Daniel made request of the king, and he appointed Shadrach, Meshach and Abed-nego over the administration of the province of Babylon, while Daniel was at the king's court.*

Because Daniel had fulfilled the king's demand, Nebuchadnezzar worshiped him and offered incense offerings to him. This was his way of worshiping God whom Daniel represented. Nebuchadnezzar made some spiritual progress. He recognized Daniel's God as being the greatest god; however, he did not recognize God as the only god. The king was still a polytheist.

The king kept his promise of reward to the one who would meet his demand. He made Daniel governor of the province called Babylon. Out of all the provinces of the kingdom this would have been the most important one, for it would have contained the capital city of Babylon. He also made Daniel head over all the wise men.

Daniel displayed great character. In his hour of exaltation he did not forget his three friends. At his request, the king appointed them to actually administrate the province of Babylon. This freed Daniel to work at the king's court.

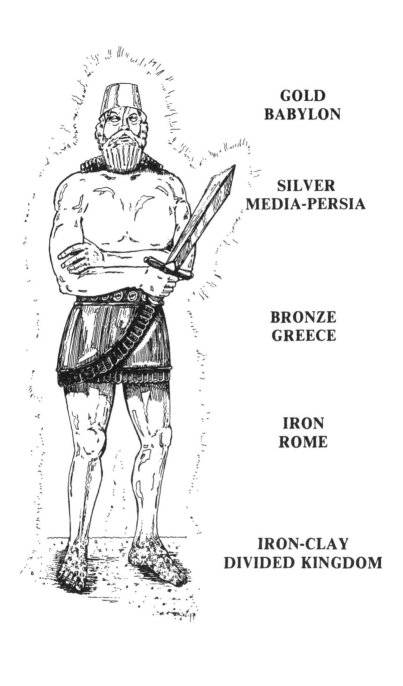

**GOLD**
**BABYLON**

**SILVER**
**MEDIA-PERSIA**

**BRONZE**
**GREECE**

**IRON**
**ROME**

**IRON-CLAY**
**DIVIDED KINGDOM**

# GOD'S RULE OVER GENTILE PUNISHMENT DEMONSTRATED

## NEBUCHADNEZZAR'S IMAGE (3:1-7)

*Nebuchadnezzar the king made an image of gold, the height of which was sixty cubits and its width six cubits; he set it up on the plain of Dura in the province of Babylon. Then Nebuchadnezzar the king sent word to assemble the satraps, the prefects and the governors, the counselors, the treasurers, the judges, the magistrates and all the rulers of the provinces to come to the dedication of the image that Nebuchadnezzar the king had set up. Then the satraps, the prefects and the governors, the counselors, the treasurers, the judges, the magistrates and all the rulers of the provinces were assembled for the dedication of the image that Nebuchadnezzar the king had set up; and they stood before the image that Nebuchadnezzar had set up. Then the herald loudly proclaimed: "To you the command is given, O peoples, nations and men of every language, that at the moment you hear the sound of the horn, flute, lyre, trigon, psaltery, bagpipe, and all kinds of music, you are to fall down and worship the golden image that Nebuchadnezzar the king has set up. But whoever does not fall down and worship shall immediately be cast into the midst of a furnace of blazing fire." Therefore at that time, when all the peoples heard the sound of the horn, flute, lyre, trigon, psaltery, bagpipe, and all kinds of music, all the peoples, nations and men of every language fell down and worshiped the golden image that Nebuchadnezzar the king had set up.*

Sometime after Daniel had interpreted the king's dream, Nebuchadnezzar had a huge image made on the plain of Dura. The image probably was human in form. It stood approximately ninety feet high and was nine feet wide.[1] No doubt the height included a large base on which the image stood. Years ago an archaeologist named Oppert discovered large mounds called the mounds of Dura some twelve miles south, southeast of Hillah.[2] One mound was a brick structure forty-five feet long on each side and twenty feet high. Oppert claimed that it had the appearance of a pedestal of a huge image — possibly the image of Daniel 3.[3]

Nebuchadnezzar probably built this image to represent the world power that he had built and to honor the Babylonian gods whom he thought had given him his power. No doubt he got the idea for his image from the image in the dream of chapter 2. However, whereas only the head of the image in the dream was made of gold, Nebuchadnezzar had this image made entirely of gold. This was an expression of rebellion against God's revelation. Through this image of gold the king was saying: "I don't care what the God of heaven has said. My kingdom of Babylon will not fall to another Gentile kingdom. It will rule throughout the times of the Gentiles."

Nebuchadnezzar commanded all the chief officers of the kingdom to be present at the dedication of the image. Daniel's three friends, Shadrach, Meshach and Abed-nego, were present, but Daniel was not. Evidently he was somewhere else in the kingdom on the king's business.

At the dedication a herald commanded everyone to fall on his face to the ground and to worship the image at a given signal. There were to be no exceptions to this command. Refusal to worship would be regarded as treason and would bring immediate punishment — death in a furnace of blazing fire. The kings of Babylon were noted for roasting alive people who disobeyed their commands (Jer. 29:22).

Once again the Jewish youths were faced with a dilemma. If they were to worship the image, they would thereby violate the first two of God's ten commandments. This would bring the wrath of God upon them. But if they were to refuse to worship the image, they would experience the king's fury. The pressure upon them was great, and they had to make their decision quickly.

Shadrach, Meshach and Abed-nego made the right decision. They chose in favor of God. When the signal was given, all the pagans of the kingdom fell down and worshiped the image, but the three Jewish young men continued to stand. Once again they refused to sacrifice the truth of God on the altar of expediency.

## DANIEL'S FRIENDS ACCUSED (3:8-12)

*For this reason at that time certain Chaldeans came forward and brought charges against the Jews. They responded and said to Nebuchadnezzar the king: "O king, live forever! You yourself, O king, have made a decree that every man who hears the sound of the horn, flute, lyre, trigon, psaltery, and bagpipe, and all kinds of music, is to fall down and worship the golden image. But whoever does not fall down and worship shall be cast into the midst of a furnace of blazing fire. There are certain Jews whom you have appointed over the administration of the province of Babylon, namely Shadrach, Meshach, and Abed-nego. These men, O king, have disregarded you; they do not serve your gods or worship the golden image which you have set up."*

Immediately some of the Chaldeans reported the insubordination of the Jewish youths to Nebuchadnezzar. Typical of the Gentiles, their anti-Semitism began to show. No doubt they were jealous of the high positions to which these Jews had been appointed.

The Chaldeans charged Shadrach, Meshach and Abed-nego with ingratitude and rebellion against the king. They indicated that, although the king had graciously honored these conquered Jews with high positions, they in turn dishonored him and his gods. The Chaldeans offered the following proof of their charge: the Jews refused to worship the king's image.

# DANIEL'S FRIENDS TRIED (3:13-18)

*Then Nebuchadnezzar in a rage and anger gave orders to bring Shadrach, Meshach, and Abed-nego; then these men were brought before the king. Nebuchadnezzar responded and said to them, "Is it true, Shadrach, Meshach and Abed-nego, that you do not serve my gods or worship the golden image that I have set up? Now if you are ready, at the moment you hear the sound of the horn, flute, lyre, trigon, psaltery, and bagpipe, and all kinds of music, to fall down and worship the image that I have made, very well. But if you will not worship, you will immediately be cast into the midst of a furnace of blazing fire; and what god is there who can deliver you out of my hands?" Shadrach, Meshach and Abed-nego answered and said to the king, "O Nebuchadnezzar, we do not need to give you an answer concerning this. If it be so, our God whom we serve is able to deliver us from the furnace of blazing fire; and He will deliver us out of your hand, O king. But even if He does not, let it be known to you, O king, that we are not going to serve your gods or worship the golden image that you have set up."*

The Chaldean accusation accomplished its intended goal. Nebuchadnezzar flew into a rage and demanded that the Jewish youths be brought before him. To his credit he asked them if the Chaldean charge were true, thereby giving the Jews opportunity to deny the accusation. The king offered them a second chance to obey his command, thereby proving their loyalty, but he repeated the original threat should they disobey again. Nebuchadnezzar boasted of the certainty of the Gentile punishment which would be administered — the furnace would be so hot that no god would be able to deliver them. Without realizing it, through that boast the king had afforded the God of heaven a splendid opportunity to display His sovereign power.

When Shadrach, Meshach and Abed-nego answered the king, "We do not need to give you an answer concerning this," they were not being arrogant. They were not saying, "We don't have to tell you anything." Instead, they were admitting that the charge against them was true; therefore, no defense or apology needed to be made.[4]

Realizing that this pagan king could never comprehend the reason for their stand, Daniel's friends gave up all attempts to justify their disobedience to the king. Instead, they simply entrusted themselves to God. They declared that, if it were God's purpose to deliver them, He would deliver them; however, if it were not God's purpose to deliver them, they still would not offend Him by obeying the king's command. Here were saints who exercised implicit faith in God.

# DANIEL'S FRIENDS SENTENCED (3:19-20)

*Then Nebuchadnezzar was filled with wrath, and his facial expression was altered toward Shadrach, Meshach and Abed-nego. He answered by giving orders to heat the furnace seven times more than it was usually heated. And he commanded certain valiant warriors who were in his army to tie up Shadrach, Meshach and Abed-nego, in order to cast them into the furnace of blazing fire.*

Nebuchadnezzar's pride could not tolerate this challenge to his sovereignty by foreigners whom he had conquered. His face became distorted with rage. He commanded the furnace to be heated seven times more intense than normal and his strongest men to bind the Jews and cast them in. These were precautions to prevent any possibility of escape or rescue.

# DANIEL'S FRIENDS PUNISHED (3:21-23)

*Then these men were tied up in their trousers, their coats, their caps and other clothes, and were cast into the midst of the furnace of blazing fire. For this reason, because the king's command was urgent and the furnace had been made extremely hot, the flame of the fire slew those men who carried up Shadrach, Meshach and Abed-nego. But these three men,*

*Shadrach, Meshach and Abed-nego, fell into the midst of the
furnace of blazing fire still tied up.*

The Babylonian furnaces were like modern limekilns with
an opening at the top, through which materials could be
dumped, and a large opening at the bottom for withdrawing
burned substances.[5] The top opening was approached by an
incline plane.[6]

Three things should be noted about the punishment.
First, Shadrach, Meshach and Abed-nego were thrown into
the furnace with highly flammable clothing. Second, the fire
in the furnace was such a raging inferno that it killed the
soldiers when they got close enough to cast in the Jews.
Third, the Jews were bound so well that they could not move
when they were dropped into the fire. All three points
emphasize the miracle about to take place.

## DANIEL'S FRIENDS DELIVERED (3:24-27)

*Then Nebuchadnezzar the king was astounded and stood up in
haste; he responded and said to his high officials, "Was it not
three men we cast bound into the midst of the fire?" They
answered and said to the king, "Certainly, O king." He answered
and said, "Look! I see four men loosed and walking about in the
midst of the fire without harm, and the appearance of the fourth
is like a son of the gods!" Then Nebuchadnezzar came near to
the door of the furnace of blazing fire; he responded and said,
"Shadrach, Meshach and Abed-nego, come out, you servants of
the Most High God, and come here!" Then Shadrach, Meshach
and Abed-nego came out of the midst of the fire. And the
satraps, the prefects, the governors and the king's high officials
gathered around and saw in regard to these men that the fire had
no effect on the bodies of these men nor was the hair of their
head singed, nor were their trousers damaged, nor had the smell
of fire even come upon them.*

Nebuchadnezzar sat opposite the large bottom opening of
the furnace. He personally wanted to watch this sure
punishment wreak its havoc on these foreign upstarts.

However, the king was not prepared for what he was about to see. As he peered into the furnace the king saw something which astonished him so much that he jumped up and questioned his counselors. He wanted to make sure that his eyes were not playing tricks on him.

Five things startled Nebuchadnezzar. First, there were four persons instead of three in the furnace. Second, not one of the persons was bound. Third, all four persons were walking around in the fire — none was lying down. Fourth, all four persons were unhurt. Fifth, the fourth person looked like "a son of the gods."[7]

The Babylonians believed that their gods had sons.[8] Thus, when Nebuchadnezzar said that the fourth person in the furnace looked like a son of the gods, this was his pagan way of saying that the fourth person looked like a divine or supernatural being.[9] Later (v. 28) the king said that God sent His angel, but it should be noted that the Aramaic word translated *angel* was also used for *deity*.[10] It is the conviction of the present writer that the fourth person in the fiery furnace was the Son of God, Jesus Christ, in a preincarnate appearance, sent by God to deliver miraculously His three faithful saints.

Realizing that his purpose had been defeated by divine intervention, Nebuchadnezzar summoned Shadrach, Meshach and Abed-nego out of the furnace, calling them servants of the Most High God. Once more he was impressed with the God of Israel — the God who sovereignly overruled Gentile punishment — but he still didn't recognize Him as the only God.

The large group of officials who were present eagerly gathered around Daniel's friends to examine them. This group would form a reliable body of witnesses to the miracle. They observed four evidences of God's miraculous power. First, no bodies were blistered. Second, no hair was singed. Third, no clothing was scorched. Fourth, there was no smell of smoke on the Jews. God had overwhelmingly demonstrated that there was a God who could deliver these sons of Israel out of the king's hands.

# NEBUCHADNEZZAR'S REACTION (3:28-30)

*Nebuchadnezzar responded and said, "Blessed be the God of Shadrach, Meshach, and Abed-nego, who has sent His angel and delivered His servants who put their trust in Him, violating the king's command, and yielded up their bodies so as not to serve or worship any god except their own God. Therefore, I make a decree that any people, nation or tongue that speaks anything offensive against the God of Shadrach, Meshach and Abed-nego shall be torn limb from limb and their houses reduced to a rubbish heap, inasmuch as there is no other god who is able to deliver in this way." Then the king caused Shadrach, Meshach and Abed-nego to prosper in the province of Babylon.*

Nebuchadnezzar praised God for delivering Shadrach, Meshach and Abed-nego. He also praised these men for their stalwart faith and devotion to their God. The king decreed terrible punishment for anyone who dared to speak anything against the God of Israel. He admitted that this God was more powerful than any other, but he still did not declare Him the only God. The king promoted Daniel's friends even more.

# LESSONS TO BE LEARNED

Several lessons should be learned from this amazing incident. First, although human government is ordained of God (Rom. 13:1-7), governmental authorities can abuse their God-given power by commanding things contrary to God. Nebuchadnezzar did this when he commanded the worship of the image. Second, when human government commands something contrary to what God commands, the saint of God must obey God rather than man. Shadrach, Meshach and Abed-nego did this when they refused to worship the image. Third, when the saint of God disobeys human government in order to obey God, he must take the consequences of disobeying the government no matter what the results. Daniel's friends did this when they were cast into the furnace. In this instance God chose to deliver them, because deliverance suited His sovereign purpose. God does not choose to deliver His saints in every instance, however. It is at times such as these that the saint must recognize the fact that he exists, not for his benefit, but for God's. Fourth, if the saint survives government's punishment, he is not to advocate overthrow of the government because it abused its power. After Shadrach, Meshach and Abed-nego were delivered by God, they continued to serve the king who had punished them. They did not demonstrate against him, nor did they start a movement to overthrow him.

# 4

# GOD'S RULE OVER GENTILE KINGS DEMONSTRATED

## NEBUCHADNEZZAR'S ROYAL PROCLAMATION (4:1-3)

*Nebuchadnezzar the king to all the peoples, nations, and men of every language that live in all the earth: "May your peace abound! It has seemed good to me to declare the signs and wonders which the Most High God has done for me. How great are His signs, and how mighty are His wonders! His kingdom is an everlasting kingdom, and His dominion is from generation to generation.*

After the events recorded in this chapter had taken place, Nebuchadnezzar had a royal proclamation about them circulated. He did this in order to teach all his people the lesson which God had taught him — the fact that the Most High God has a kingdom that is sovereign over man and will last forever in contrast to man's kingdoms. Chapter four records this royal proclamation. This makes the chapter unique, for it contains what the king himself wrote.

There are two lines of evidence which indicate that the words of this chapter are actually Nebuchadnezzar's. First, the literary style of chapter four resembles the style of Nebuchadnezzar's ancient inscriptions.[1] Second, the character of the king revealed in this chapter agrees with ancient descriptions of the man.[2]

## NEBUCHADNEZZAR'S DREAM (4:4-18)

*"I, Nebuchadnezzar, was at ease in my house and flourishing in my palace. I saw a dream and it made me fearful; and these*

*fantasies as I lay on my bed and the visions in my mind kept alarming me. So I gave orders to bring into my presence all the wise men of Babylon, that they might make known to me the interpretation of the dream. Then the magicians, the conjurers, the Chaldeans, and the diviners came in, and I related the dream to them; but they could not make its interpretation known to me. But finally Daniel came in before me, whose name is Belteshazzar according to the name of my god, and in whom is a spirit of the holy gods; and I related the dream to him, saying, 'O Belteshazzar, chief of the magicians, since I know that a spirit of the holy gods is in you and no mystery baffles you, tell me the visions of my dream which I have seen, along with its interpretation. Now these were the visions in my mind as I lay on my bed: I was looking, and behold, there was a tree in the midst of the earth, and its height was great. The tree grew large and became strong, and its height reached to the sky, and it was visible to the end of the whole earth. Its foliage was beautiful and its fruit abundant, and in it was food for all. The beasts of the field found shade under it, and the birds of the sky dwelt in its branches, and all living creatures fed themselves from it. I was looking in the visions in my mind as I lay on my bed, and behold, an angelic watcher, a holy one, descended from heaven. He shouted out and spoke as follows: "Chop down the tree and cut off its branches, strip off its foliage and scatter its fruit; let the beasts flee from under it, and the birds from its branches. Yet leave the stump with its roots in the ground, but with a band of iron and bronze around it in the new grass of the field; and let him be drenched with the dew of heaven, and let him share with the beasts in the grass of the earth. Let his mind be changed from that of a man, and let a beast's mind be given to him, and let seven periods of time pass over him. This sentence is by the decree of the angelic watchers, and the decision is a command of the holy ones, in order that the living may know that the Most High is ruler over the realm of mankind, and bestows it on whom He wishes, and sets over it the lowliest of men." This is the dream which I, King Nebuchadnezzar, have seen. Now you, Belteshazzar, tell me its interpretation, inasmuch as none of the wise men of my kingdom is able to make known to me the interpretation; but you are able, for a spirit of the holy gods is in you.'*

During the latter half of Nebuchadnezzar's reign, while he rested from wars and prospered at home, he had a dream that disturbed him greatly.[3] Nebuchadnezzar called in the different classes of wise men, told them the content of the dream and asked them to interpret. This time the wise men could not even make up an interpretation. They were at a total loss concerning the meaning of the dream.

Finally Daniel was brought in. Nebuchadnezzar realized that only a supernatural being could interpret this dream, and Daniel had demonstrated before that he had contact with such a being.

The king related the content of his dream to Daniel. In the dream he saw a tree that had vast branches and bore much fruit. It grew up to heaven and provided lodging and food for beasts, birds and people. Then a holy "watcher" came from heaven and commanded that the tree be cut down with only the stump left in the ground. The stump was to be bound with a band of iron and bronze, and its heart was to be changed from a man's to a beast's until seven times had passed. The purpose of the "watcher's" command was as follows: to teach the living that the Most High God rules in the kingdom of men, gives it to whomever He wills and sets up over it the lowliest of men.

The "watcher" of the dream probably was an angel.[4] The angel's statement to the effect that God sets up the lowliest of men over the kingdom of men would have caught Nebuchadnezzar's attention. The word translated *lowliest* means *humblest*, and Nebuchadnezzar's father, Nabopolassar, claimed to be of very humble origin.[5] In one of his inscriptions Nabopolassar referred to himself as follows: "in my littleness, the son of a nobody," "of me, the insignificant, who among men was not visible," "I, the weak, the feeble."[6] These statements implied that Nabopolassar was not of royal birth and did not count in society before he became king.[7]

## DANIEL'S REACTION TO THE DREAM (4:19)

*"Then Daniel, whose name is Belteshazzar, was appalled for a*

*while as his thoughts alarmed him. The king responded and said, 'Belteshazzar, do not let the dream or its interpretation alarm you.' Belteshazzar answered and said, 'My lord, if only the dream applied to those who hate you, and its interpretation to your adversaries!*

As Daniel became aware of the meaning of the dream, he was shocked and greatly perplexed. He did not want to tell the bad meaning of the dream to the king, but Nebuchadnezzar insisted. Daniel expressed the wish that the tragedy portrayed by the dream would fall upon the king's enemies instead of upon the king.

## DANIEL'S INTERPRETATION OF THE DREAM (4:20-27)

*'The tree that you saw, which became large and grew strong, whose height reached to the sky and was visible to all the earth, and whose foliage was beautiful and its fruit abundant, and in which was food for all, under which the beasts of the field dwelt and in whose branches the birds of the sky lodged — it is you, O king; for you have become great and reached to the sky and your dominion to the end of the earth. And in that the king saw an angelic watcher, a holy one, descending from heaven and saying, "Chop down the tree and destroy it; yet leave the stump and its roots in the ground, but with a band of iron and bronze around it in the new grass of the field, and let him be drenched with the dew of heaven, and let him share with the beasts of the field until seven periods of time pass over him"; this is the interpretation, O king, and this is the decree of the Most High, which has come upon my lord the king: that you be driven away from mankind, and your dwelling place be with the beasts of the field, and you be given grass to eat like cattle and be drenched with the dew of heaven; and seven periods of time will pass over you, until you recognize that the Most High is ruler over the realm of mankind, and bestows it on whomever He wishes. And in that it was commanded to leave the stump with the roots of the tree, your kingdom will be assured to you after you recognize that it is Heaven that rules. Therefore, O king, may my advice be pleasing to you: break away now from your sins by doing righteousness,*

*and from your iniquities by showing mercy to the poor, in case there may be a prolonging of your prosperity.'*

Daniel declared that the tree in the dream represented King Nebuchadnezzar. Just as the tree grew to great size and strength, so Nebuchadnezzar's influence and power had spread throughout the known world.

God's representation of Nebuchadnezzar as a large tree that provided food and lodging for all was very fitting for at least two reasons. First, in several of his inscriptions Nebuchadnezzar had boasted about the peaceful shelter and abundance of food that he had provided for his subjects through Babylon. Indeed, in these boasts he used language descriptive of a tree when referring to his rule through Babylon. In one inscription he said, "The produce of the lands, the product of the mountains, the bountiful wealth of the sea within her I received. Under her everlasting shadow I gathered all men in peace. Vast heaps of grain beyond measure I stored up within her."[8] In another inscription he declared, "Under her everlasting shadow I gathered all men in peace. A reign of abundance, years of plenty I caused to be in my land."[9]

Second, as a result of military campaigns that took him several times through the forests of Lebanon, Nebuchadnezzar became greatly captivated by the huge cedar trees of that land. This attitude was reflected in one of his inscriptions where he described the trees as follows: "mighty cedars, tall and strong, of costly value, whose dark forms towered aloft, the massive growth of Lebanon."[10] Indeed, in his inscriptions Nebuchadnezzar boasted that he personally had cut down some of these huge trees with his own hands. He even had a picture of himself cutting a cedar inscribed on stone.[11] One gets the impression that the king exalted in the fact that he could cut down such a towering giant of strength.

This king who delighted in cutting down trees would

himself be cut down. Daniel indicated that the cutting down and destruction of the tree in the dream symbolized the fact that God would remove Nebuchadnezzar from his office of king. Just as the stump in the dream was bound with a metal band, so God would bind the king with a form of mental illness. This illness would cause the king to act like a wild beast. He would be driven from the palace to live outdoors in all kinds of weather. His hair would get matted from the dew. He would eat grass like other wild animals. This madness would last until Nebuchadnezzar would acknowledge the fact that Jehovah is sovereign over the kingdom of men.

The fact that the stump of the tree was left in the ground in the dream was God's promise to Nebuchadnezzar that He would restore his kingdom to him after his acknowledgment of God's sovereignty.

After giving the interpretation, Daniel urged Nebuchadnezzar to repent of his past ways. The king had gravely mistreated many of his subjects, especially during his great building projects (Hab. 2:11-13), so Daniel made a plea for him to rule justly. Daniel did not promise escape from the judgment portrayed in the dream, but he did say that perhaps God would increase the king's time of peace and prosperity as a result of his repentance.

## THE FULFILLMENT OF THE DREAM (4:28-33)

*"All this happened to Nebuchadnezzar the king. Twelve months later he was walking on the roof of the royal palace of Babylon. The king reflected and said, 'Is this not Babylon the great, which I myself have built as a royal residence by the might of my power and for the glory of my majesty?' While the word was in the king's mouth, a voice came from heaven, saying, 'King Nebuchadnezzar, to you it is declared: sovereignty has been*

*removed from you, and you will be driven away from mankind,
and your dwelling place will be with the beasts of the field. You
will be given grass to eat like cattle, and seven periods of time
will pass over you, until you recognize that the Most High is
ruler over the realm of mankind, and bestows it on whomever
He wishes.' Immediately the word concerning Nebuchadnezzar
was fulfilled; and he was driven away from mankind and began
eating grass like cattle, and his body was drenched with the dew
of heaven, until his hair had grown like eagles' feathers and his
nails like birds' claws.*

In his royal proclamation Nebuchadnezzar confessed that
the tragedy portrayed in the dream really happened. The
fulfillment began one year after the dream had been given.
At that time the king was walking on the roof of the royal
palace of Babylon looking out over the great capital city.
There were several royal palaces in Babylon, but this was
probably the one which had the famous Hanging Gardens
upon its roof. That particular palace stood on high ground
and was centrally located.[12] From that vantage point the
king would have a magnificent view of the entire city.

As Nebuchadnezzar looked out over the city of Babylon
his heart swelled with pride. He boasted that he himself had
made Babylon the greatest city on earth by the might of his
own power. He declared that he had made Babylon so
magnificent in order to glorify himself. The king was on an
ego trip. He was a classic illustration of man exalting over
what he can do himself apart from God.

From a purely human viewpoint, Nebuchadnezzar had
good reason to boast. He probably was the greatest builder
in ancient times.[13] Forty-nine building inscriptions of this
king have been uncovered thus far.[14] Most of the bricks
recovered from ancient Babylon bear this inscription: "I am
Nebuchadnezzar, King of Babylon."[15] He himself declared
that his heart impelled him to build.[16]

Nebuchadnezzar rebuilt the old palace of his father, then
built two more palaces.[17] He built seventeen religious

temples in Babylon and its suburb, Borsippa.[18] He completed the two great walls that surrounded the city.[19] The outer wall was wide enough for chariots to pass each other on its top.[20] The king installed great fortifications to protect the city and had canals dug from one end of the city to another to facilitate commerce.[21]

One of Nebuchadnezzar's most splendid projects was the magnificent Ishtar Gate. This was a double gateway through the walls of the city. The walls of this gate were covered with bulls and four-legged dragons in high relief. The approach to the gate was between strong fortress walls on which were rows of lions in relief and covered with brightly colored tiles.[22]

The king's greatest building feat was the Hanging Gardens. One of Nebuchadnezzar's wives, the princess of Media, grew homesick for the mountains of her homeland. In order to satisfy her, the king had mountains built on the roof of the royal palace complex. These mountains were planted with trees and other kinds of plants. An ingenious hydraulic machine system was devised to lift water from the Euphrates River to water the elevated gardens.[23] These Hanging Gardens became so famous that the Greeks named them one of the Seven Wonders of the World.[24]

The fact that Nebuchadnezzar was very proud of Babylon is indicated by one of his prayers to Marduk: "Like dear life I love thy exalted lodging place: in no place have I made a town more glorious than thy city of Babylon."[25]

While Nebuchadnezzar's proud words of boasting were proceeding from his mouth, a voice from heaven interrupted with God's sentence of judgment: "King Nebuchadnezzar, to you it is declared: sovereignty has been removed from you." Immediately the mental illness foretold in the dream seized the king, and he was driven from his throne to live in the open fields like a wild animal.

The illness with which Nebuchadnezzar was stricken is

called lycanthropy.[26] Although this insanity causes a person to act like a wild beast, the victim still retains an inner consciousness.[27] This would explain the king's ability to change his attitude while suffering this madness.

## NEBUCHADNEZZAR'S REACTION (4:34-37)

*"But at the end of that period, I, Nebuchadnezzar, raised my eyes toward heaven, and my reason returned to me, and I blessed the Most High and praised and honored Him who lives forever; for His dominion is an everlasting dominion, and His kingdom endures from generation to generation. And all the inhabitants of the earth are accounted as nothing, but He does according to His will in the host of heaven and among the inhabitants of earth; and no one can ward off His hand or say to Him, 'What hast Thou done?' At that time my reason returned to me. And my majesty and splendor were restored to me for the glory of my kingdom, and my counselors and my nobles began seeking me out; so I was re-established in my sovereignty, and surpassing greatness was added to me. Now I Nebuchadnezzar praise, exalt, and honor the King of heaven, for all His works are true and His ways just, and He is able to humble those who walk in pride."*

When Nebuchadnezzar finally recognized that he was in a situation that he could not control, he swallowed his pride and humbly looked to God. He gave forth praise with an excellent expression of the sovereignty of God. God immediately restored his kingdom to him. As a result, Nebuchadnezzar exalted and honored God all the more. Now that he had recognized God's sovereignty, he called God "King."

## HISTORICAL NOTATIONS

Skeptics have scoffed at the account of Nebuchadnezzar's mental illness in Daniel. They have claimed that it is preposterous to believe that such a thing happened to such a mighty king. However, a Greek writer named Megasthenes, who lived from 312-280 B.C., related an interesting story that had been told to him by the Chaldeans. According to this story, after he had completed military conquests, Nebuchadnezzar "was possessed by some god or other" while on the roof of his palace.[28] The story also talked about a man driven through the desert where wild beasts sought their food — "a lonely wanderer among the rocks and ravines."[29] Although this story differed in several respects from the account in Daniel, the similarities were strong enough to have prompted the conclusion that the Chaldean account to Megasthenes was a perversion of what actually happened to Nebuchadnezzar.[30]

In addition, it is interesting to note that for four years Nebuchadnezzar's name disappeared from the historical and governmental records of Babylon. It reappeared for a brief time before the king died.[31]

# 5

# GOD'S RULE OVER GENTILE DEFENSES DEMONSTRATED

## HISTORICAL BACKGROUND

King Nebuchadnezzar died on October 7, 562 B.C.[1] After three other men had ruled and passed from the scene, Nabonidus became king of Babylon in 556 B.C.[2] Nabonidus was king when the events of Daniel chapter five took place.

## BELSHAZZAR'S FEAST (5:1-4)

*Belshazzar the king held a great feast for a thousand of his nobles, and he was drinking wine in the presence of the thousand. When Belshazzar tasted the wine, he gave orders to bring the gold and silver vessels which Nebuchadnezzar his father had taken out of the temple which was in Jerusalem, in order that the king and his nobles, his wives, and his concubines might drink from them. Then they brought the gold vessels that had been taken out of the temple, the house of God which was in Jerusalem; and the king and his nobles, his wives, and his concubines drank from them. They drank the wine and praised the gods of gold and silver, of bronze, iron, wood, and stone.*

The opening verse of chapter five presents the reader with two problems. First, who was Belshazzar? For centuries this was a mystery, for available Babylonian records mentioned no king named Belshazzar. As a result, critics said that this proved that the Book of Daniel was historically inaccurate. However, during the 1920's, the deciphering of more recently discovered Babylonian documents solved the mystery. These documents indicated that Belshazzar was the son of King Nabonidus.[3]

The second problem is this: if Nabonidus was king during the events of Daniel chapter five, then why does verse one call Belshazzar "king?" Some Babylonian documents solved this problem as well. They indicated the following: in 555 B.C. Nabonidus marched an army westward to conquer rebels who had revolted against Babylonian rule since the death of Nebuchadnezzar. Before he left Babylon on this expedition, Nabonidus entrusted "kingship" to his oldest son, Belshazzar.[4] Through time Nabonidus built a royal palace in the distant town of Tema in the heart of the Arabian penisula, and he settled there.[5] While Nabonidus maintained the title of king in Arabia, Belshazzar exercised kingship in Babylon. Many letters and business documents indicated that Belshazzar functioned as the real authority.[6] Thus, a co-regency situation existed, and Daniel was accurate in calling Belshazzar "king."

Belshazzar put on a huge feast for one thousand of his subordinate officials. On such occasions it was an Oriental custom for the king to sit at a separate table on an elevated platform where all the guests could see him.[7] It would appear that during the course of the feast a drinking bout began, led by the king.

After Belshazzar got drunk he commanded that the sacred vessels of Jehovah's Temple, which his "father" Nebuchadnezzar had brought from Jerusalem to place in the Temple of Marduk, be brought to the banquet hall. (The word "father" does not mean that Belshazzar was the immediate son of Nebuchadnezzar. In ancient Oriental languages the word "father" was used loosely to refer to any male ancestor.[8] In fact, in this instance it was used to refer to a legal ancestor, for Belshazzar was a legal, not a physical, descendent of Nebuchadnezzar.[9])

It was Belshazzar's intention that Jehovah's vessels be

used as drinking vessels by himself, the nobles, his wives and his concubines. The concubines were the inferior class of women from the royal harem. They probably were present for the purpose of a sexual orgy.[10] Once the vessels were brought to the banquet hall, they were used to praise the Babylonian gods and to produce more drunken debauchery. Belshazzar could not have chosen a more degrading way to desecrate the vessels of the God who hates idolatry, drunkenness and immorality.

Since the Temple of Marduk held vessels of the gods of other conquered peoples, it seems rather obvious that Belshazzar had a definite reason for choosing the vessels of the God of Israel. Why did he single out the vessels of Jehovah for this defiling purpose? The answer to this question is found in several factors of historical background.

First, it is a fact that Belshazzar as a boy had association with the royal court of Nebuchadnezzar. He would have been about fourteen years of age when Nebuchadnezzar died.[11] Thus, he would have been old enough to have known and understood some of God's dealings with Nebuchadnezzar. Indeed, in verse twenty-two Daniel clearly stated that Belshazzar knew these things. Through his association with the royal court, Belshazzar no doubt heard about Nebuchadnezzar's image dream recorded in chapter two — the dream in which the God of Israel revealed that the kingdom of Babylon would fall to Medo-Persia. Of course, in order for the kingdom to fall, its capital city of Babylon would also have to fall. Thus, Belshazzar probably knew about Jehovah's prophecy concerning Medo-Persia's conquest of Babylon.

Second, several ancient sources indicate that Medo-Persian troops, under the leadership of King Cyrus, had conquered the areas surrounding the city of Babylon perhaps as much as four months prior to the night of

Belshazzar's feast.[12] This would explain why so many Babylonian officials were in the capital city at this time. The officials had fled to this fortress city before the advancing Medo-Persian army. Thus, it is a fact that, on the night that Belshazzar defiled Jehovah's vessels, the very people whom God had foretold would take Babylon were encamped outside that city's walls. Babylon was cut off from outside help.

Third, it is a fact that Nebuchadnezzar had made Babylon into "the world's mightiest fortress."[13] The outer wall surrounding the city was so thick that no battering rams or other instruments of warfare were sufficient to knock it down. The presence of a second inner wall and numerous fortress towers and ramparts made any attempt to scale the walls suicidal. As a result, Babylon appeared to be impregnable.[14] Belshazzar and his officials were convinced that the Medo-Persians could not penetrate those amazing defenses.

But even if Babylon's defenses could keep the Medo-Persians outside the city, how long could the Babylonians inside hold out against a blockade? They would need food and water to survive. The Babylonians had solved this problem as well. The walls of Babylon had been built over the Euphrates River. Thus, that river flowed through the city at all times, providing a constant source of fresh water.[15] In anticipation of a blockade by Medo-Persia, the Babylonians had supplied the city with enough food to maintain its population for more than twenty years.[16] Ancient historians indicate that, in light of all these great preparations, the people of Babylon laughed at the siege of their city by Medo-Persia.[17]

In light of these historical factors, it seems rather obvious that Belshazzar decided to desecrate the sacred vessels of Jehovah for one major reason — to show his utter contempt for the God of Israel and His prophecy concerning the fall of

Babylon. The king was so confident of Babylon's defenses that he decided to challenge this God. His defiling of the vessels was his way of shaking his fist at God and saying: "You have said that Babylon will fall to the Medo-Persians who are now encamped outside our gates. I am declaring to you that Babylon will not fall. Its defenses are impregnable. No one will be able to take it. My actions show you what I think of you and your prophecy." Once again a pagan king was providing God with a splendid opportunity to demonstrate His sovereignty.

## THE HANDWRITING ON THE WALL (5:5-9)

*Suddenly the fingers of a man's hand emerged and began writing opposite the lampstand on the plaster of the wall of the king's palace, and the king saw the back of the hand that did the writing. Then the king's face grew pale, and his thoughts alarmed him; and his hip joints went slack, and his knees began knocking together. The king called aloud to bring in the conjurers, the Chaldeans and the diviners. The king spoke and said to the wise men of Babylon, "Any man who can read this inscription and explain its interpretation to me will be clothed with purple, and have a necklace of gold around his neck, and have authority as third ruler in the kingdom." Then all the king's wise men came in, but they could not read the inscription or make known its interpretation to the king. Then King Belshazzar was greatly alarmed, his face grew even paler, and his nobles were perplexed.*

During the course of the debauched revelry that challenged God, the fingers of a mysterious, unattached hand suddenly appeared out of nowhere and wrote something on the wall of the banquet hall. When Belshazzar saw this unique happening, he became sober in a hurry. The color drained from his face; he became painfully disturbed, and fear gripped him so strongly that his hip joints let loose, and his knees began knocking together. This was a drastic change for the man who moments earlier had been defying almighty God.

The king screamed for his wise men. When they appeared, Belshazzar promised three rewards to anyone who could read and interpret the writing. The first reward would be purple clothing which was worn by royalty.[18] The second reward would be a gold neck chain. In Babylon such chains could be worn only if given by a king.[19] The third reward would involve the authority to be third ruler in the kingdom. This third reward reflected the co-regency which existed at that time with Nabonidus and Belshazzar being first and second rulers.

None of the wise men could read or interpret the writing. Their failure caused mass confusion for the king and his officials.

## THE QUEEN MOTHER'S SUGGESTION (5:10-12)

*The queen entered the banquet hall because of the words of the king and his nobles; the queen spoke and said, "O king, live forever! Do not let your thoughts alarm you or your face be pale. There is a man in your kingdom in whom is a spirit of the holy gods; and in the days of your father, illumination, insight, and wisdom like the wisdom of the gods were found in him. And King Nebuchadnezzar, your father, your father the king, appointed him chief of the magicians, conjurers, Chaldeans, and diviners. This was because an extraordinary spirit, knowledge and insight, interpretation of dreams, explanation of enigmas, and solving of difficult problems were found in this Daniel, whom the king named Belteshazzar. Let Daniel now be summoned, and he will declare the interpretation."*

The queen referred to in this passage may have been the widow of Nebuchadnezzar whom Nabonidus married when he became king. In ancient times it was an Oriental custom for a new king to marry widows of former kings in order to make his claim to the throne more legitimate.[20] Such a woman would have been known as queen mother and would have been highly respected.

Having heard about the confusion in the banquet hall, the queen mother entered and told the king about Daniel. It would appear that Daniel had been out of royal service for several years, due to several changes of administration since Nebuchadnezzar's death. The very fact that the queen mother knew so much about Daniel's supernatural abilities and dealings with Nebuchadnezzar would seem to indicate that this woman had had a close relationship with that king. In light of Daniel's past record of interpreting dreams and solving problems, the queen mother urged that he be summoned to read and interpret the writing.

## DANIEL'S APPEARANCE
## BEFORE THE KING (5:13-16)

*Then Daniel was brought in before the king. The king spoke and said to Daniel, "Are you that Daniel who is one of the exiles from Judah, whom my father the king brought from Judah? Now I have heard about you that a spirit of the gods is in you, and that illumination, insight, and extraordinary wisdom have been found in you. Just now the wise men and the conjurers were brought in before me that they might read this inscription and make its interpretation known to me, but they could not declare the interpretation of the message. But I personally have heard about you, that you are able to give interpretations and solve difficult problems. Now if you are able to read the inscription and make its interpretation known to me, you will be clothed with purple and wear a necklace of gold around your neck, and you will have authority as the third ruler in the kingdom."*

Belshazzar called Daniel to the banquet hall, rehearsed what he had heard about his unique abilities and past accomplishments, and promised him the same three rewards which he had promised to the wise men, if he could read and interpret the writing.

# DANIEL'S ADMONITION
# TO THE KING (5:17-24)

*Then Daniel answered and said before the king, "Keep your gifts for yourself, or give your rewards to someone else; however, I will read the inscription to the king and make the interpretation known to him. O king, the Most High God granted sovereignty, grandeur, glory, and majesty to Nebuchadnezzar your father. And because of the grandeur which He bestowed on him, all the peoples, nations, and men of every language feared and trembled before him; whomever he wished he killed, and whomever he wished he spared alive; and whomever he wished he elevated, and whomever he wished he humbled. But when his heart was lifted up and his spirit became so proud that he behaved arrogantly, he was deposed from his royal throne, and his glory was taken away from him. He was also driven away from mankind, and his heart was made like that of beasts, and his dwelling place was with the wild donkeys. He was given grass to eat like cattle, and his body was drenched with the dew of heaven, until he recognized that the Most High God is ruler over the realm of mankind, and that he sets over it whomever He wishes. Yet you, his son, Belshazzar, have not humbled your heart, even though you knew all this, but you have exalted yourself against the Lord of heaven; and they have brought the vessels of His house before you, and you and your nobles, your wives and your concubines have been drinking wine from them; and you have praised the gods of silver and gold, of bronze, iron, wood and stone, which do not see, hear or understand. But the God in whose hand are your life-breath and your ways, you have not glorified. Then the hand was sent from Him, and this inscription was written out.*

Daniel refused the king's rewards to make it clear that he wouldn't invent a reading and interpretation in order to get personal gain. Before doing what Belshazzar desired, Daniel gave the king a history lesson. He recounted how the God of Israel had made Nebuchadnezzar a great king, but then humbled him with mental illness because of his excessive pride and until he recognized the sovereign rule of God.

Daniel applied the example of Nebuchadnezzar to Belshazzar. In spite of the fact that Belshazzar knew about the humiliation of Nebuchadnezzar, he hadn't learned humility from it. Instead, through his desecration of the vessels of Jehovah, he had exalted himself against the very God who had abased Nebuchadnezzar. In light of the precedent of Nebuchadnezzar, Belshazzar should have glorified the God who sovereignly controlled his life breath. Because of Belshazzar's arrogant contempt, God sent the mysterious hand to write its ominous message.

## DANIEL'S READING
## AND INTERPRETATION
## OF THE WRITING (5:25-28)

*"Now this is the inscription that was written out: 'MENE, MENE, TEKEL, UPHARSIN.' This is the interpretation of the message: 'MENE' — God has numbered your kingdom and put an end to it. 'TEKEL' — you have been weighed on the scales and found deficient. 'PERES' — your kingdom has been divided and given over to the Medes and Persians."*

In compliance with the king's request, Daniel read and interpreted the writing. The reading was as follows: MENE, MENE, TEKEL, UPHARSIN. Later, when Daniel interpreted the writing, he used a different form of the last word. He used PERES instead of UPHARSIN. UPHARSIN was the same word as PERES, but its form differed "both by the addition of the prefix 'U,' which is the conjunction 'and,' and also by the use of the plural ending."[21]

To say the least, the interpretation that Daniel gave was not encouraging for Belshazzar and his officials. The word MENE meant *numbered* or *reckoned*.[22] It indicated that God had numbered the days of Belshazzar's kingdom and had reckoned that those days had come to their end.[23] This word had been written twice to emphasize the certainty of the end of Belshazzar's kingdom.[24]

The word TEKEL meant *weighed*.[25] It signified that God

had weighed Belshazzar in His balance and had found him
deficient in moral worth.[26] Since the king did not measure
up to God's standard, he was not fit to continue ruling.

The word PERES meant *broken* or *divided*.[27] It implied
that God had determined to shatter Belshazzar's kingdom
and to give it to Medo-Persia. This was so certain to happen
that Daniel spoke of it as an already accomplished fact.

## BELSHAZZAR'S RESPONSE (5:29)

*Then Belshazzar gave orders, and they clothed Daniel with
purple and put a necklace of gold around his neck, and issued a
proclamation concerning him that he now had authority as the
third ruler in the kingdom.*

Whereas Belshazzar had shown contempt for God's
earlier prophecy concerning the fall of the Babylonian
kingdom, he now believed this most recent prophecy that
bore the same message. Perhaps this change of attitude was
due to the fact that this latest prophecy had been delivered in
written form. The Babylonians believed that the decrees of
the gods existed in written form.[28]

Because Belshazzar believed this prophecy, he rewarded
Daniel with the three promised rewards. Daniel now
accepted the rewards, for he knew that the king properly
understood his motives in reading and interpreting the
writing.

## THE END OF BELSHAZZAR
## AND BABYLON (5:30)

*That same night Belshazzar the Chaldean king was slain.*

More than once God had foretold the fall of Babylon to
Medo-Persia. Opposed to those prophecies were the amazing defenses of Babylon. With the Medo-Persian troops

outside the gates of that city, the sovereignty of the God of Israel was now on the line before the pagan Babylonians. Could Daniel's God cause the fulfillment of His prophecies in spite of the defenses that were thought to be impregnable?

King Cyrus of Medo-Persia knew that the defenses of Babylon would not permit the entrance of his troops into that city through conventional means of warfare. It was obvious that, if Babylon were to be taken, a unique strategy would have to be employed. According to more than one ancient historian, the Medo-Persians did devise a unique strategy. The key to that strategy was the position of the Euphrates River under the massive walls of the city. On the very night that the Babylonians were reveling at Belshazzar's feast, the Medo-Persians diverted the water of the Euphrates River from its normal channel under the city walls. Once the water was shallow enough to be forded, Medo-Persian soldiers entered the river channel and walked underneath the walls into the city. The Babylonians were caught by surprise. Before many of them knew what was happening, their city had fallen to the Medo-Persians without a major battle or destruction.[29]

Some of the Medo-Persian commanders led soldiers directly to the royal palace to get Belshazzar. As they attacked the Babylonian guards outside the palace gates, a great deal of noise was caused. Out of curiosity, Belshazzar ordered some of the men inside the palace to investigate the noise. As these men opened the palace gates to discover the source of the uproar, some of the Medo-Persian soldiers rushed through the gates into the palace. They headed directly for the banquet hall. Upon entering the hall they found Belshazzar standing with his sword drawn. They killed the king and many of his officials.[30] Thus, Belshazzar was slain, and the great city of Babylon fell on the night of October 13, 539 B.C.[31]

Once again God demonstrated His sovereignty. In spite of

Babylon's great defenses, it fell in one day's time just as God had foretold (cf. Isa. 47:9). The nations of the world should learn a lesson from this event – no matter how extensive or sophisticated the defenses, no nation will be able to stand when God says that it is time for it to fall.

## THE CHANGE OF RULERS (5:31)

*So Darius the Mede received the kingdom at about the age of sixty-two.*

Daniel indicated that Darius the Mede ruled the kingdom of Babylon after it fell to Medo-Persia. That statement has posed a problem. Who was Darius the Mede? Ancient documents did not record a man with this name ruling Babylon immediately after its conquest by Medo-Persia.

Two observations should be made concerning this problem. First, the name "Darius" probably was a title of honor rather than a personal name. Josephus, the ancient Hebrew historian, claimed that Darius had another name. The ancient Greek historian, Herodotus, and modern authorities on the old Persian language claim that "Darius" was a title rather than a proper name.[32] "Darius" means *holder of the scepter.*[33]

Second, scholars have disagreed concerning the identification of Darius. Most recent research, however, favors the view that he was Gubaru (Gobryas), the man whom King Cyrus appointed to be governor of Babylon. Gubaru was born in 601 B.C.; thus, as Daniel indicated, he would have been "about the age of sixty-two" when Babylon fell in 539 B.C. Gubaru's father was a Mede; thus, he too was a Mede. The area over which Cyrus appointed him governor was basically the same as that which comprised the former kingdom of Babylon.[34]

King Cyrus divided his enormous empire into twenty

provinces and appointed a governor to rule each province. Each province formerly had been an independent kingdom with its own king. Thus, each governor replaced a former king.[35] "As successor to a former king, ruling a truly enormous territory, he was in point of fact himself a monarch and was surrounded by a miniature court."[36] As a result, it has been said of Gubaru that he "ruled almost as an independent monarch."[37]

In light of this, Daniel was not stretching the truth when he referred to Darius as "king over the kingdom of the Chaldeans" (9:1). Since Darius had been appointed by the head king, Cyrus, Daniel was accurate when he wrote that Darius "received the kingdom" (5:31) and "was made king" (9:1).

6

# GOD'S RULE OVER
# GENTILE LAW DEMONSTRATED

## DANIEL'S POSITION
## UNDER DARIUS (6:1-3)

*It seemed good to Darius to appoint 120 satraps over the kingdom, that they should be in charge of the whole kingdom, and over them three commissioners (of whom Daniel was one), that these satraps might be accountable to them, and that the king might not suffer loss. Then this Daniel began distinguishing himself among the commissioners and satraps because he possessed an extraordinary spirit, and the king planned to appoint him over the entire kingdom.*

Darius was a good administrator. He appointed 120 officials under him to help him govern the former kingdom of Babylon. In accord with this statement of Daniel, the ancient Annalistic Tablet of Cyrus stated that Gubaru "appointed governors in Babylon."[1]

The king appointed three men to be heads over the 120 officials. It was the responsibility of these heads to supervise the work of the officials — especially their work of collecting taxes for Darius. Daniel was one of the three appointed heads. In spite of the fact that the rule of the kingdom had passed from the Babylonians to the Medo-Persians, God sovereignly kept Daniel in a high government position.

Daniel performed so much better than the other heads and officials that through time the new king planned to make him superior over all the others. From a human viewpoint, this was very remarkable, for by this time Daniel was at least eighty years of age. The reason Daniel performed so well was the fact that "he possessed an extraordinary spirit." In other words, God sovereignly gave him supernatural enablement.

## THE OFFICIALS' PLOT (6:4-9)

*Then the commissioners and satraps began trying to find a ground of accusation against Daniel in regard to government affairs; but they could find no ground of accusation or evidence of corruption, inasmuch as he was faithful, and no negligence or corruption was to be found in him. Then these men said, "We shall not find any ground of accusation against this Daniel unless we find it against him with regard to the law of his God." Then these commissioners and satraps came by agreement to the king and spoke to him as follows: "King Darius, live forever! All the commissioners of the kingdom, the prefects and satraps, the high officials and the governors have consulted together that the king should establish a statute and enforce an injunction that anyone who makes a petition to any god or man besides you, O king, for thirty days, shall be cast into the lions' den. Now, O king, establish the injunction and sign the document so that it may not be changed, according to the law of the Medes and Persians, which may not be revoked." Therefore King Darius signed the document, that is, the injunction.*

The other heads and officials became jealous of Daniel's favor with the king. Typical of Gentiles, they could not tolerate a Jew being in such a high position. They began to plot to get him removed from office. They carefully examined his record of government service, hoping to catch him in some point of unfaithfulness, negligence or corruption. But to their frustration, they could not find even one ground of accusation. Daniel was one politician who had been trustworthy, responsible and honest.

Daniel's untarnished government record forced his opponents to look elsewhere for something that could be used against him. Because Daniel had a reputation for being devoted to Jehovah, the God of Israel, these men decided to use the Law of God as a weapon against him. Anti-Semitism consumed them so strongly that they were driven to use any tactic necessary to get rid of Daniel.

Once these men had devised their scheme, they obtained an audience with King Darius. They told the king that all his officials had made a unanimous decision after consultation together. That statement was a lie, for Daniel had not been involved in this consultation. Their decision was this: that the king should pass and enforce a decree that anyone who would make a religious request of any god or man except the king for thirty days should be cast into the lions' den. In other words, they were suggesting that Darius should be regarded as the only representative of deity for one month.[2] The men purposely appealed to the king's vanity through this suggestion, hoping to dupe him into putting their scheme into effect.

Apparently the officials had written the suggested decree in document form before their audience with the king. The only thing needed to put the decree into effect was the king's signature on that document. The men designed it that way so that Darius would not have time to think through the results of this decree. Time was of the essence for the success of their scheme; therefore, as soon as they had presented the suggested decree, the officials pressed the king to sign the document.

The officials were anxious for the king's signature because of the unique nature of the Medo-Persian law.

> For it was a proud boast of Persia that its laws never changed, and that a royal promise or decree was irrevocable. In his edicts and judgments the king was supposed to be inspired by the god Ahura-Mazda himself; therefore the law of the realm was the Divine Will, and any infraction of it was an offense against the deity.[3]

The men knew that, once the decree was put into effect, no one, including the king himself, could revoke it. Thus, the point at issue in this incident was Medo-Persian law.

Under the pressure of the moment, King Darius allowed himself to be trapped by the officials' plot. He signed the decree, thereby making it part of the law of the Medes and Persians.

## DANIEL'S ENSNAREMENT
## BY THE PLOT (6:10-15)

*Now when Daniel knew that the document was signed, he entered his house (now in his roof chamber he had windows opened toward Jerusalem); and he continued kneeling on his knees three times a day, praying and giving thanks before his God, as he had been doing previously. Then these men came by agreement and found Daniel making petition and supplication before his God. Then they approached and spoke before the king about the king's injunction, "Did you not sign an injunction that any man who makes a petition to any god or man besides you, O king, for thirty days, is to be cast into the lions' den?" The king answered and said, "The statement is true, according to the law of the Medes and Persians, which may not be revoked." Then they answered and spoke before the king, "Daniel, who is one of the exiles from Judah, pays no attention to you, O king, or to the injunction which you signed, but keeps making his petition three times a day." Then, as soon as the king heard this statement, he was deeply distressed and set his mind on delivering Daniel; and even until sunset he kept exerting himself to rescue him. Then these men came by agreement to the king and said to the king, "Recognize, O king, that it is a law of the Medes and Persians that no injunction or statute which the king establishes may be changed."*

No doubt the officials left the king's palace with great glee. They knew that the king's decree was opposed to the Law of Daniel's God. That Law forbade idolatry, and a Jewish prayer to anyone other than Jehovah would be a form of idolatry. They were convinced that they had Daniel trapped in a dilemma of faithfulness — would this Jew be faithful to his God or to the king who favored him?

To a certain extent, Daniel could have avoided the trap quite easily. Since the decree did not say that a person had to pray during the thirty days, he could have stopped praying altogether for that month. By not praying to the king, he could avoid violating God's Law against idolatry. By not praying to God, he could avoid violating the king's decree. Daniel could have reasoned that, since his life was at stake, certainly God would not mind a prayerless life for such a short period of time.

Daniel refused to take the easy way out. He was not a fair-weather friend who would serve God only when personally convenient or when there was no price to pay. He was convinced that his daily relationship with God should take precedence over the will of man. As a result, when he learned about the decree, he continued his normal prayer practice. He went to his roof chamber and prayed to God three times a day. He didn't even avoid the open windows or pray silently in order to escape detection, and he continued to thank God in spite of the decree. Once again he was doing what was right and trusting God for the results.

The officials spied on Daniel to see if he would pray to God. When they found him praying they rushed eagerly to the king to accuse Daniel. Having gotten the king to admit that he had signed this irrevocable decree, they informed Darius that Daniel had violated it. They carefully pointed out that Daniel was a conquered foreigner — a Jew — thereby insinuating that his disobedience had been prompted by political unfaithfulness.[4]

For the first time Darius realized that he had been tricked into doing something contrary to his own desires. When he learned that his folly had caught his favorite official in a trap, he became very disturbed. The king tried desperately to undo the decree until sunset. According to Oriental custom, a punishment must be executed "on the evening of the day in which the accusation was made."[5]

The officials, being very perturbed by the king's reaction, belabored him with the fact that the decree could not be revoked. Although this reminder probably irritated Darius, the officials held tenaciously to the unchangeable nature of Medo-Persian law. It was their surety for getting rid of Daniel.

## DANIEL'S PUNISHMENT IN THE DEN (6:16-18)

*Then the king gave orders, and Daniel was brought in and cast into the lions' den. The king spoke and said to Daniel, "Your God whom you constantly serve will Himself deliver you." And a stone was brought and laid over the mouth of the den; and the king sealed it with his own signet ring and with the signet rings of his nobles, so that nothing might be changed in regard to Daniel. Then the king went off to his palace and spent the night fasting, and no entertainment was brought before him; and his sleep fled from him.*

Darius had no alternative but to have Daniel cast into the lions' den. The most he could do was express to Daniel the wish that Daniel's God would deliver him. Once again God was confronted with an opportunity to display His sovereign rule in the affairs of men. Could He rescue His faithful servant from death and thereby overrule this Medo-Persian law that no one else could revoke?

The lions' den probably was an underground cavern with an opening for air at the top and a door on the side.[6] A large stone was placed over the door. The stone was sealed first by the king to assure that the officials would not go beyond what the decree demanded in order to guarantee Daniel's death. Then the officials sealed the stone to prevent the king from interfering to rescue Daniel.[7]

Darius spent a miserable night. He was so upset that he could not eat or sleep, and he refused all entertainment.

# DANIEL'S DELIVERANCE FROM THE DEN (6:19-23)

*Then the king arose with the dawn, at the break of day, and went in haste to the lions' den. And when he had come near the den to Daniel, he cried out with a troubled voice. The king spoke and said to Daniel, "Daniel, servant of the living God, has your God, whom you constantly serve, been able to deliver you from the lions?" Then Daniel spoke to the king, "O king, live forever! My God sent His angel and shut the lions' mouths, and they have not harmed me, inasmuch as I was found innocent before Him; and also toward you, O king, I have committed no crime." Then the king was very pleased and gave orders for Daniel to be taken up out of the den. So Daniel was taken up out of the den, and no injury whatever was found on him, because he had trusted in his God.*

With great anxiety Darius rose at the crack of dawn the next day and rushed to the den. With a pitiable voice he called out a question to Daniel: "Has your God been able to deliver you from the lions?" This question reflected a pagan outlook. It implied that, if Daniel were dead, it was because his God was incapable of delivering him. The king hoped that his call would be answered by the voice of Daniel rather than the loud belching of a satisfied lion.

Daniel responded to the king by declaring that his God had sent His angel to shut the lions' mouths. As a result, the lions had not harmed Daniel. Perhaps this heavenly messenger was the Angel of Jehovah, the preincarnate Christ, who had delivered Daniel's three friends from the fiery furnace many years before. God delivered Daniel because he had not violated God's Law and had not been guilty of political unfaithfulness to the king.

With great relief Darius ordered Daniel to be brought up from the den. Evidently Daniel was drawn up through the top air opening. The king did not want to break the seals on the stone covering the door, thereby giving the officials opportunity to accuse him of rescuing Daniel during the night. Daniel was examined carefully. Not even one scratch could be found on this servant of Jehovah. God had honored Daniel's faith and had demonstrated His sovereignty over Gentile law.

## THE OFFICIALS' PUNISHMENT (6:24)

*The king then gave orders, and they brought those men who had maliciously accused Daniel, and they cast them, their children, and their wives into the lions' den; and they had not reached the bottom of the den before the lions overpowered them and crushed all their bones.*

Darius had those officials who had accused Daniel thrown into the lions' den together with their wives and children. This was their punishment for trying to kill a faithful government official and for tricking the king into doing something that caused him much turmoil. Herodotus and other ancient writers indicated that Persian rulers executed all of a man's relatives when he committed a crime worthy of death.[8] This was a sure way of preventing assassination attempts upon the life of the king by disgruntled relatives in future years.

These victims were dropped into the den through the top air opening. Before they hit the bottom of the den, the lions attacked and began their terrible work of devouring them. Daniel recorded the ferocity of the lions to emphasize the truly miraculous nature of his own deliverance. His survival was not due to the lions being overly fed or too old to care about him.

## DARIUS' NEW DECREE (6:25-27)

*Then Darius the king wrote to all the peoples, nations and men of every language who were living in the land: "May your peace*

*abound! I make a decree that in all the dominion of my kingdom
men are to fear and tremble before the God of Daniel; for He is
the living God and enduring forever, and His kingdom is one
which will not be destroyed, and His dominion will be forever.
He delivers and rescues and performs signs and wonders in
heaven and on earth, who has also delivered Daniel from the
power of the lions."*

Darius was so impressed with the miracle Jehovah had
performed that he issued a new decree. In this decree he
commanded all his subjects to have reverent respect for
Daniel's God. He described Jehovah as the living God who
is eternal and forever sovereign and who works all sorts of
miracles. This was a remarkable decree from a pagan ruler,
but it should be noted that Darius did not call Jehovah the
only God.

## THE SUMMARY STATEMENT
## CONCERNING DANIEL (6:28)

*So this Daniel enjoyed success in the reign of Darius and in the
reign of Cyrus the Persian.*

Daniel concluded chapter six with a summary statement
similar to the one that ended chapter one. In spite of enemies
who tried to destroy him, Daniel survived and prospered in
the contemporary reigns of Darius, the subking, and Cyrus,
the head king. This was a great testimony concerning God's
sovereign care of His servant.

# GOD'S RULE OVER GENTILE EMPIRES DEMONSTRATED AGAIN

## A NOTE OF EXPLANATION

In chapters seven through twelve Daniel related dreams or visions that he received during the later years of his life. Some of these were received before the events of chapters five and six. At least one was received after those events.

## DANIEL'S DREAM (7:1-14)

*In the first year of Belshazzar king of Babylon Daniel saw a dream and visions in his mind as he lay on his bed; then he wrote the dream down and related the following summary of it. Daniel said, "I was looking in my vision by night, and behold, the four winds of heaven were stirring up the great sea. And four great beasts were coming up from the sea, different from one another. The first was like a lion and had the wings of an eagle. I kept looking until its wings were plucked, and it was lifted up from the ground and made to stand on two feet like a man; a human mind also was given to it. And behold, another beast, a second one, resembling a bear. And it was raised up on one side, and three ribs were in its mouth between its teeth; and thus they said to it, 'Arise, devour much meat!' After this I kept looking, and behold, another one, like a leopard, which had on its back four wings of a bird; the beast also had four heads, and dominion was given to it. After this I kept looking in the night visions, and behold, a fourth beast, dreadful and terrifying and extremely strong; and it had large iron teeth. It devoured and crushed, and trampled down the remainder with its feet; and it was different from all the beasts that were before it, and it had ten horns. While I was contemplating the horns, behold, another horn, a little one, came up among them, and three of the first horns were pulled out by the roots before it; and behold, this horn possessed eyes like the eyes of a man, and a mouth uttering great boasts. I kept looking until thrones were set up, and the Ancient of Days took His seat; His vesture was like white snow, and the hair of His head like pure wool. His throne was ablaze with flames, its wheels were a burning fire. A river of fire was flowing and coming out from before Him; thousands upon thousands were attending Him, and myriads upon myriads were standing before Him; the court sat, and the books were opened. Then I kept looking because of the sound of the boastful words which the horn was speaking; I kept looking until the beast was slain, and its body was destroyed and given to the burning fire. As for the rest of the beasts, their dominion was taken away, but an extension of life was granted to them for an appointed period of time. I kept looking in the night visions, and behold, with the clouds of heaven One like a Son of Man was coming, and He came up to the Ancient of Days and was presented before Him. And to Him was given dominion, glory and a kingdom, that all the peoples, nations, and men of every language might serve Him. His dominion is an everlasting dominion which will not pass away; and His kingdom is one which will not be destroyed.*

The dream or vision recorded by Daniel in chapter seven was received during the first year that Belshazzar reigned over Babylon. The year probably was 553 B.C.[1] Thus, the dream came to Daniel between the events recorded in chapters four and five.

In his dream Daniel saw the four winds of heaven stir up the great sea into a chaotic state. Since this was a dream, the things Daniel saw were symbols of real things. When the sea is used symbolically in the Bible, it usually represents the world of nations (Isa. 17:12-13; Rev. 17:1, 15).[2] Thus, this chaotic sea represented the world of nations in turmoil.

Daniel saw four great beasts come up from the sea one after the other. It will be seen that these four beasts represented four great Gentile kingdoms — the same kingdoms which were represented by the great image of Nebuchadnezzar's dream in chapter two. All four kingdoms rose from the same chaotic world conditions, but each was different from the other three.

The first beast was a lion with eagle's wings. This represented the kingdom of Babylon that was in existence when Daniel received this dream. It corresponded to the head of gold of the image of chapter two. Winged lions were practically the national symbol of ancient Babylon. Sculptures of huge winged lions stood at the entrances of Babylonian royal palaces.[3] Interestingly, the Scriptures compared Nebuchadnezzar, the greatest king of Babylon, to a lion (Jer. 50:17) and an eagle (Ezek. 17:3, 12). Lions and eagles have been regarded as the kings of the beasts and fowl, and wings often signify swiftness of movement. Thus, a winged lion was a fitting representation of Babylon in its swift conquest of many peoples as it made itself the king of nations during the first part of Nebuchadnezzar's reign (Hab. 1:6, 8).

As Daniel watched the lion, eventually its wings were plucked off; it was made to stand on its hind feet like a human being, and a human heart was given to it. After Nebuchadnezzar had been humbled by God through lycanthropy, he and his kingdom stopped conquering and became more humane in their treatment of their subjects.

The second beast that rose from the sea was a bear. This represented the kingdom of Medo-Persia. Its counterpart in the image of chapter two was the breast and arms of silver. Just as a bear is more massive in size but slower moving than a lion, so Medo-Persia became much larger as a kingdom than was Babylon, and the Medo-Persian army was noted for its huge size but slower movements.[4]

The bear had one side raised higher than the other side. As noted in chapter two, the Medo-Persian kingdom was a partnership. It is a fact of history that through time the

Persians gained the ascendancy of authority and power over the Medes.

The bear had three ribs in its mouth. These probably represented Lydia, Babylon and Egypt — three other great kingdoms that were conquered by Medo-Persia.[5] In spite of these great conquests, the bear was commanded to devour even more. Medo-Persia was noted for its insatiable desire to conquer more.

Medo-Persia replaced Babylon as the great world power in 539 B.C.

The third beast that Daniel saw was a leopard with four wings and four heads. This represented the kingdom of Greece and was parallel to the belly and thighs of bronze of the image in Nebuchadnezzar's dream. Leopards are noted for their ability to run fast (Hab. 1:8). Since the two wings on the lion represented swiftness of movement, four wings on the leopard signified that concept even more. Thus, the major thing emphasized by the third beast was swiftness of conquest. Under Alexander the Great, Greece conquered the known  world faster than any other ancient power. Alexander had the fastest moving army known. In eight years time the Greeks marched and conquered more than 11,000 miles of territory from Greece in the west to India in the east.[6]

Alexander died on June 13, 323 B.C. when only thirty-two years of age.[7] After his death his kingdom was divided into four parts by four leading generals.[8] These four divisions were represented by the four heads of the leopard.

Greece broke the back of Medo-Persian power by 331 B.C.

The fourth beast that rose from the sea was a nondescript animal. This represented the Roman Empire. It corresponded to the legs of iron and feet and toes of iron and clay of the image in chapter two. This beast was so terrifying and ferocious that there was no living animal which could represent it. The major thing emphasized concerning this beast was its overwhelming destructive power. With iron teeth it devoured and crushed everything in its way and trampled all else under its feet. This was an apt description of the Roman Empire, for it was able to crush and shatter the ancient world in an unparalleled way through its great military might.

Ten horns rose out of the beast's head. While Daniel carefully observed these ten horns, an eleventh little horn rose up among them. As this little horn pushed its way up from the beast's head, it uprooted three of the ten horns. The little horn had human eyes, indicating that it possessed human intelligence and personality.[9] It also possessed a mouth which spoke boastful things.

The interpretation of the ten horns and the little horn was given to Daniel later (vv. 23-24). Daniel was told that all the horns represented kings. In chapter two it was noted that in ancient times kings and kingdoms were synonymous with each other. Thus, the ten horns represented ten kings and their kingdoms, and the little horn represented an eleventh king and his kingdom.[10]

When the interpretation of Daniel's dream is examined later, it will be seen that the little horn (eleventh king) represented the Antichrist — the ultimate man of the future who will be the greatest expression of man trying to rule the world apart from God.

It should be noted that the little horn rose up "among" the ten horns (v. 8). This indicated that the Antichrist would begin to come to power while the ten kings or kingdoms represented by the ten horns would be present on earth.

According to verses seven and eight, the ten horns and the little horn rose out of and were part of the fourth beast — the Roman Empire. This indicated that the Roman Empire would experience three stages of history — first, the beast stage; second, the ten horn or ten kingdom stage; and third, the little horn or Antichrist stage.

Rome succeeded Greece as world ruler by 146 B.C.

Up to this point Daniel's dream focused upon an earthly scene — the succession of Gentile world kingdoms on earth. At verse nine the dream shifted from an earthly to a heavenly scene. Daniel saw judgment thrones set up in heaven (the expression "the court sat" in verse ten literally means *the judgment sat*[11]). Once the court was arranged, God sat upon His throne to administer judgment.

God was called the Ancient of Days, indicating that He has lived throughout the entire course of history as an eyewitness of all the deeds of human beings and kingdoms. He is one Judge who does not have to rely upon secondhand testimony as the basis for His judgments. Thus, His judgments are accurate.

In this symbolic representation of God, His clothing was like white snow and His hair was like pure wool. These items signified the purity or righteousness of God (Isa. 1:18). He is a Judge who is untainted by corruption. Thus, His judgments are absolutely just.

God's throne consisted of fire, and a river of fire flowed out from before Him. Fire represented the glory of God, and the glory of God always signified the special presence of God — sometimes His presence to administer judgment (Num. 14:10-12; Dt. 4:24). In this instance it certainly signified God's special presence on a throne to administer judgment.

Daniel saw "a thousand thousands" plus "ten thousand times ten thousand" angels serving God and standing before His throne waiting to receive His commands which they would obey.[12] Centuries later the Apostle John saw this same angelic throng around the throne of God in heaven (Rev. 5:11). Ten thousand times ten thousand equals one hundred million, but there were thousands upon thousands more. These statements by Daniel and John were intended to relate the fact that there are innumerable hosts of angels serving God (Heb. 12:22). In Daniel's dream the angels were prepared to execute the sentence of judgment which God would pronounce.

As the judgment session began, books were opened. The Scriptures indicate that God keeps records of human deeds (Rev. 20:12). Since verses eleven and twelve declared that it was the little horn and the four beasts which were to be judged, it would appear that the books in Daniel's dream contained the deeds of the Antichrist and the four great Gentile world kingdoms. These would receive the exact judgment they deserved.

While God in heaven prepared to administer judgment, Antichrist (the last great ruler of the Roman Empire) kept spouting off his boastful claims on earth. Finally God executed judgment upon the Antichrist and his Roman Empire. This fourth Gentile kingdom was totally consumed by the fire of God's judgment.

Verse twelve served as a contrast with verse eleven. When each of the first three Gentile world kingdoms (represented by the first three beasts) fell, they were not totally destroyed. They were absorbed into the next world kingdom which conquered them and continued to exist as part of the new expression of Gentile world dominion. In that sense Babylon, Medo-Persia and Greece would continue to live for the entire period of time that God appointed for Gentile world dominion. By contrast, the fourth kingdom (the Roman Empire) would be totally destroyed in its fall. It would not be made part of the kingdom that would succeed it.

Since Babylon, Medo-Persia and Greece continued to exist as part of the Roman Empire, the judgment of Rome would be their judgment as well. Thus, God's total destruction of Antichrist's Roman Empire would also be God's total destruction of Gentile world dominion. Never again would it dominate the world. This concept corresponds with what was portrayed in the dream of chapter two. When the stone crushed the image's feet (which represented the Roman Empire), it thereby crushed the entire image (which represented the whole course of Gentile world dominion, including Babylon, Medo-Persia, Greece and Rome).

It should be noted that this judgment seen by Daniel is not the Great White Throne Judgment seen by John in Revelation 20:11-15. According to Daniel 7:9-14, the judgment seen by Daniel would take place *before* Messiah's kingdom would be established; but, according to Revelation 20:1-15, the Great White Throne Judgment would take place at least one thousand years *after* Messiah's kingdom had been established. The judgment of Daniel 7 is the judgment of Gentile world dominion, but the Great White Throne Judgment of Revelation 20 is the final judgment of all unsaved people of all ages of history. Some of the judgment seen by Daniel will fall upon the Roman Empire during the coming Tribulation Period (Rev. 6-18), but it will reach its grand climax at the second coming of Christ (Rev. 19:11-21).

As Daniel continued to watch his dream, a new person appeared in the heavenly scene. This person was "like a Son of Man" and was "coming with the clouds of heaven." The expression "a Son of Man" indicated that this person was human, an offspring of man, but the word "like" implied that He was more than just human. Several Old Testament passages declared that the clouds are the chariot of God (Ps. 104:3; Isa. 19:1). Thus, the fact that this Son of Man was coming "with the clouds of heaven" indicated that He also was deity. Daniel was seeing a person who was deity incarnated in human form.

Who was this unique person? Ancient Jewish writers believed that this was the Messiah.[13] Jesus Christ believed the same, for, when He presented Himself as the Messiah during His first coming, He frequently claimed to be the Son of Man who would come with the clouds of heaven (Mt. 24:30; 25:31; 26:64). The Apostle John recognized Jesus Christ as this person (Rev. 1:7, 13; 14:14).

Messiah approached the Ancient of Days and was presented before Him. The language demands the conclusion that the Messiah and the Ancient of Days were two distinct persons. Thus, two separate divine beings, God the Father and God the Son, appeared in Daniel's dream.

Messiah appeared before the Ancient of Days for a definite purpose — to receive the rule of the earth. Now that God in His sovereignty had ended Gentile world dominion, the earth needed a new kingdom with a new king. Just as God had foretold in Psalm 2, He sovereignly gave all the peoples and nations of the earth to His Son to rule over as King. The fifth and final kingdom that replaced the four Gentile kingdoms was the Kingdom of God. In contrast with the Gentile kingdoms, the Kingdom of God would last forever (for one thousand years on the present earth and for eternity on the new eternal earth). This part of Daniel's dream corresponded to the stone that became a great mountain and filled the earth in the dream of chapter two.

It is important to note that, although Daniel's dream portrayed things as if they had already happened, most of the dream (from the second beast on) was prophetic. Daniel received the dream while Babylon (represented by the first beast) was in power. The rule of Medo-Persia, Greece, Rome and the Kingdom of God were yet future. The fact that God could foretell the future course of world dominion with complete accuracy demonstrates His sovereignty over kingdoms and history. The fact that Messiah's reception of the rule of the earth was the last thing portrayed in Daniel's dream implied that the Kingdom of God would be the goal or grand climax of world history.

Some Bible students have concluded that the Kingdom of

God portrayed in Daniel's dream was established by Jesus Christ during His first coming. At least two things are opposed to that view. First, according to Daniel 7:13-14, Messiah would receive the kingdom in conjunction with His coming with the clouds of heaven. It is a fact that Jesus did not come with the clouds of heaven in His first coming. Instead, He came through birth by a young Jewess (Gal. 4:4). Second, Jesus placed the fulfillment of Daniel 7:13-14 at His second coming. In Matthew 24:29-31 Jesus said that it would be after the Tribulation of the future that the sign of the Son of Man would appear in the sky and the tribes of the earth would see the Son of Man coming on the clouds of the sky with power and great glory. Again He said that when the Son of Man would come in His glory, and all the angels with Him, then He would sit on His glorious throne (Mt. 25:31). When Jesus was on trial, He told the men of the Sanhedrin that they would see the Son of Man coming on the clouds of heaven hereafter (Mt. 26:64). For reasons such as these, it can be concluded that the Kingdom of God in Daniel 7 will be established by Christ in conjunction with His second coming.

## THE INTERPRETATION OF DANIEL'S DREAM (7:15-27)

*"As for me, Daniel, my spirit was distressed within me, and the visions in my mind kept alarming me. I approached one of those who were standing by and began asking him the exact meaning of all this. So he told me and made known to me the interpretation of these things: 'These great beasts, which are four in number, are four kings who will arise from the earth. But the saints of the Highest One will receive the kingdom and possess the kingdom forever, for all ages to come.' Then I desired to know the exact meaning of the fourth beast, which was different from all the others, exceedingly dreadful, with its teeth of iron and its claws of bronze, and which devoured, crushed, and trampled down the remainder with its feet, and the meaning of*

*the ten horns that were on its head, and the other horn which came up, and before which three of them fell, namely, that horn which had eyes and a mouth uttering great boasts, and which was larger in appearance than its associates. I kept looking, and that horn was waging war with the saints and overpowering them until the Ancient of Days came, and judgment was passed in favor of the saints of the Highest One, and the time arrived when the saints took possession of the kingdom. Thus he said: 'The fourth beast will be a fourth kingdom on the earth, which will be different from all the other kingdoms, and it will devour the whole earth and tread it down and crush it. As for the ten horns, out of this kingdom ten kings will arise; and another will arise after them, and he will be different from the previous ones and will subdue three kings. And he will speak out against the Most High and wear down the saints of the Highest One, and he will intend to make alterations in times and in law; and they will be given into his hand for a time, times, and half a time. But the court will sit for judgment, and his dominion will be taken away, annihilated and destroyed forever. Then the sovereignty, the dominion, and the greatness of all the kingdoms under the whole heaven will be given to the people of the saints of the Highest One; His kingdom will be an everlasting kingdom, and all the dominions will serve and obey Him.'*

Daniel was so troubled over what his dream could mean that he asked one of God's angels to give him the exact interpretation of it. The angel gave a general interpretation of the entire dream first. He declared that the four beasts represented four kings (or, as noted earlier, four kingdoms) which were earthly in origin. Obviously these four kingdoms would rule the earth for sometime, but eventually the rule of the earth would be given to the saints of God. Once the saints would receive that rule, they would possess it forever.

Several observations should be made concerning the saints ruling the world. First, this last part of the general interpretation was related to the last part of Daniel's dream, where the future Kingdom of God was established on earth as the result of the Ancient of Days giving the rule of the earth to Messiah. This means, then, that the saints will be given the rule of the earth when the future Kingdom of God is established on earth. Second, the saints will not bring in or establish the future Kingdom of God. Instead, they will "receive" it. It is God who will establish the Kingdom of God through His Messiah. Messiah will be the King, and the saints will be subrulers under the King (Mt. 19:28; Rev. 20:4-6). Third, it is the saints, not the unsaved, who will receive the Kingdom of God. Other passages indicate that only saved individuals will be allowed to enter the future Kingdom of God when it is established. The unsaved who will be living at Christ's second coming will be executed (Ezek. 20:33-38; Mal. 3:2-3, 5; Mt. 13:40-43, 47-50; 24:37-40; 25:31-46).

Having received the general interpretation of his dream, Daniel requested a precise interpretation of the nondescript fourth beast, its ten horns and its eleventh or little horn. Here Daniel mentioned two items concerning the little horn that he had not recorded earlier. First, the horn that began little in size became larger than its associate horns. Second, this horn waged war against the saints and overpowered them. It did this until God judged it and its kingdom on behalf of the saints and gave them the rule of the earth through Messiah.

In response to Daniel's request, the angel stated that the fourth beast represented a fourth kingdom on the earth. It would be different from the first three kingdoms. This difference was due to its overwhelming destructive power. As noted earlier, this kingdom was the Roman Empire.

The angel indicated that the Roman Empire would pass through three stages of history. The first stage could be called the beast or conquering stage (v. 23). Rome would devour and crush a much greater area than the earlier three kingdoms would. This first stage was descriptive of the ancient Roman Empire.

The second stage could be called the ten horn or ten kingdom stage (v. 24). The angel declared that eventually ten kings would rise out of the fourth kingdom. Since the ten horns were part of the fourth beast (v. 7), this meant that eventually the Roman Empire would have ten rulers or would consist of a ten nation confederation. As noted in chapter two, since the ancient Roman Empire never consisted of a ten nation confederation, this form of the fourth kingdom must be future. Sometime in the future the Roman Empire will be revived in the form of a ten nation confederation.

The third stage of Rome's history could be called the little horn or Antichrist stage (v. 24). The angel stated that, after the ten nation confederation would be formed, an eleventh king would rise up. Since he would rise up "among" the ten kings (v. 8), it appears that he would belong to the ten nation confederation. This king would be different from the other ten in the following way: whereas the other ten kings would be content to be equals in their confederation, this king would not be content to be an equal. He would be driven by the compulsion to be the chief ruler of the confederation. Therefore, as he would be rising to power, he would overthrow three of the ten kings, thereby making himself more powerful than any of the other seven. The symbolism used for this king in Daniel's dream was very fitting. Just as the eleventh horn originally was smaller than the other ten, because it rose up after they were already present, so the eleventh king initially would have less power than the ten kings, because he would begin his rise to power after they would be established in their positions of rule. Just as the eleventh horn became larger in appearance than the other ten, so the eleventh king would become more powerful than the ten kings. It is apparent, then, that the future Revived Roman Empire will become dominated by the rule of one man.

Once this king comes to full power he will become very bold. The angel indicated that he would do three things (v.

25). First, he would "speak out against the Most High." He would blaspheme God. In Daniel 11:36, where he was called "the king," it was stated that he would "speak monstrous things against the God of gods." John declared that there would be "given to him a mouth speaking arrogant words and blasphemies; . . . And he opened his mouth in blasphemies against God, to blaspheme His name and His tabernacle" (Rev. 13:5-6).

The word translated "against" in Daniel 7:25 literally means *at the side of.*[14] This king would blaspheme by trying to elevate himself to the level of God. He would claim deity for himself and would try to speak with the same authority as God speaks. Daniel 11:36 said that he would "exalt and magnify himself above every god." Paul wrote the following concerning him: "who opposes and exalts himself above every so-called god or object of worship, so that he takes his seat in the temple of God, displaying himself as being God" (2 Th. 2:4). John indicated that this man would be worshiped by many people (Rev. 13:4, 8, 12, 15).

Second, this king would wage war against the saints of God. He would be able to persecute the believers of his time quite successfully (v. 21). John wrote: "And it was given to him to make war with the saints and to overcome them" (Rev. 13:7). John indicated that many of these saints would be martyred for refusing to worship this king (Rev. 20:4). The angel told Daniel that the saints would be given into this king's hand for "a time, times, and half a time." A time (one time) plus times (the simple plural implies two times) plus one-half time equals three and one-half times. How long would three and one-half times be? In Revelation 13:5-7, where John talked about this king blaspheming God and waging war against the saints, the apostle declared: "and authority to act for forty-two months was given to him" (v. 5). Forty-two months is three and one-half years. Thus, the three and one-half times would be three and one-half years.

Once this king would begin to blaspheme God by claiming deity for himself and demanding that he be worshiped as God, he would have three and one-half years to persecute the saints of God. When Daniel 9:27 will be examined, it will be seen that this king will claim deity for himself three and one-half years before the second coming of Christ. In light of this, it can be concluded that this persecution of the saints will take place during the last three and one-half years before Christ's second coming.

The third bold action of this king would be as follows: he would "intend to make alterations in times and in law." God is the One who determined the times, such as day and night, days, seasons, years, the length of human lives, when nations and kings would exist and rule and when the Gentiles would dominate the world (Gen. 1:14; 8:22; Ps. 31:15; Dan. 2:21; 7:12; Lk. 21:24; Acts 1:7; 17:26). He also is the One who determined moral law and natural law and instituted human government to bring law and order to society (Gen. 2:24; 9:5-6; Job 38; Isa. 40:12-13, 26; Rom. 13:1-7). Times and law are the instruments by which God regulates the affairs of man on earth. The angel did not relate what specific alterations in times and law this king would intend to make. It is apparent, however, that he will be determined to exercise authority over two areas that are the exclusive right of God. No doubt he will attempt this in order to support his claim of deity.

From the description given of this king, it is obvious that he will be the ultimate man, the greatest expression of the man-centered mania which has been driving man to reject God's rule since the fall of man in Eden (2 Th. 2:3-4, 7-8). He will be the one whom John called Antichrist (1 Jn. 2:18).

In verses twenty-six and twenty-seven the angel interpreted the heavenly judgment scene recorded by Daniel in verses nine through fourteen. The angel made it clear that the Antichrist would not be able to carry on his ungodly rule

forever. When God's time for judging Gentile world
dominion would arrive, then Antichrist's kingdom would be
taken away from him, and that kingdom (the Roman
Empire) would be annihilated and destroyed forever. This
would be the end of the Roman Empire and Gentile world
dominion. Other passages dealing with the judgment of the
Antichrist and his kingdom make it clear that this judgment
will take place at the second coming of Christ at the end of
the Tribulation (2 Th. 2:1-8; Rev. 19:11-21). This indicates
again that the Revived Roman Empire with its ten nation
confederation and rule of Antichrist is yet future.

The final part of the angel's interpretation dealt with the
coming of the Kingdom of God. The angel said that the
kingdom, the dominion and the greatness of all the
kingdoms under the whole heaven would be given to the
saints of God. As noted earlier, this would happen through
the Messiah. God would give the rule of the earth to Him.
He would establish the Kingdom of God on earth and would
make the saints subrulers under Him (Rev. 20:1-6). In
contrast with Antichrist's Roman Empire, Messiah's
kingdom would last forever. All the nations of the world
would serve and obey Messiah in that kingdom.

Two things should be noted concerning the Kingdom of
God presented in Daniel 7. First, both the dream and the
interpretation dealt with historical events in chronological
order. Since they dealt with the total destruction of the
Roman Empire and Gentile world dominion before they
introduced the Kingdom of God, they implied that there
would be no coexistence of the Roman Empire with the
Kingdom of God. The Roman Empire would be completely
gone before the Kingdom of God would be established. In
light of this, the Kingdom of God portrayed in Daniel 7 was
not established by Christ during His first coming, for, as
noted in chapter two, the Roman Empire continued to exist
for several centuries after Christ's first coming. The

Kingdom of God of Daniel 7 will not be established until Christ's second coming.

Second, the language of Daniel 7 indicated that the future Kingdom of God would be an earthly, political kingdom, not just a spiritual kingdom. If the Kingdom of God were simply the rule of Christ in the hearts of saints in the present or eternity future, then the Kingdom of God would consist of something that possesses and rules the saints. It would not consist of something that the saints receive, possess and rule. But Daniel 7:18 stated that the saints would "receive" and "possess" the kingdom; verse twenty-seven declared that the saints would "be given" the kingdom, and verse twenty-two indicated that the saints would take "possession" of the kingdom. Along these same lines, Jesus taught that the kingdom is something "prepared for" the saints (Mt. 25:34), and John declared that the saints would rule the kingdom with Christ (Rev. 20:4, 6).

In addition, it is important to note precisely what would be given to the saints to possess and rule. Verse twenty-seven indicated that the saints would be given "the greatness of the kingdoms under the whole heaven." The expression *under heaven* is used throughout Scripture to refer to what is earthly in nature or belongs to the earth (Gen. 6:17; 7:19; Job 28:24; 37:3; Eccl. 1:13; 2:3; Dan. 9:12; Acts 2:5). Thus, the Kingdom of God that would be given to the saints would include the greatness of the earthly domain. The saints would possess and rule the earthly domain which belonged to the nations of the entire earth.

## DANIEL'S RESPONSE TO THE DREAM (7:28)

*"At this point the revelation ended. As for me, Daniel, my thoughts were greatly alarming me and my face grew pale, but I kept the matter to myself."*

At this point the interpretation of the dream ended. Daniel was greatly disturbed by the dream, no doubt because of the troublesome times of the future which it portrayed. He was so upset that his color drained from his face. Although the dream troubled him, he did not try to shove it out of his mind. He kept it in his heart probably to ponder it for days to come.

## A CONCLUDING SUMMARY

The dream of Daniel 7 portrayed the same thing as the dream of Daniel 2 — the course of Gentile world dominion from the time of Babylon to the second coming of Christ. During this extensive period of history, the Gentiles would have supremacy in the world, and Israel and Jerusalem would be trodden down by the Gentiles. It is the period that Jesus called *The Times of The Gentiles* (Lk. 21:24).

Daniel 2 portrayed Gentile world dominion as it appears to rebellious man; therefore, it presented that dominion as a brilliant, glorious human image. Daniel 7 portrayed it as it appears to God; therefore, it presented Gentile dominion's true, inward nature — that of wild, voracious beasts.

**LION**
**BABYLON**

**BEAR**
**MEDIA-PERSIA**

**LEOPARD**
**GREECE**

**FIERCE BEAST**
**ROME**

**TEN HORNS**
**DIVIDED KINGDOM**

# PART II:

## GOD'S SOVEREIGN RULE OVER ISRAEL DEMONSTRATED

### Chapters 8-12

# 8

# GOD'S CHASTENING OF ISRAEL IN THE NEAR FUTURE

## A NOTE OF EXPLANATION

Now that the section dealing with God's rule over the Gentiles was completed, Daniel returned to using the Hebrew language. In light of the disturbing dream or vision of chapter seven, Daniel probably was wrestling with the following question: if three more Gentile kingdoms were to dominate the world after Babylon, what would happen to Israel during that extensive period of time? In response to that question, God gave Daniel revelations concerning the future of Israel. Daniel recorded these revelations in chapters eight through twelve. Since these chapters were concerned primarily with Israel, Daniel wrote them in the language of Israel.

## DANIEL'S SECOND VISION INTRODUCED (8:1)

*In the third year of the reign of Belshazzar the king a vision appeared to me, Daniel, subsequent to the one which appeared to me previously.*

The vision recorded by Daniel in chapter eight was received during the third year of Belshazzar's reign over Babylon. The year probably was 551 B.C. [1] Daniel made it clear that this vision came after the one recorded in chapter seven.

# THE CONTENT OF THE VISION (8:2-14)

*And I looked in the vision, and it came about while I was looking, that I was in the citadel of Susa, which is in the province of Elam; and I looked in the vision, and I myself was beside the Ulai Canal. Then I lifted up my gaze and looked, and behold, a ram which had two horns was standing in front of the canal. Now the two horns were long, but one was longer than the other, with the longer one coming up last. I saw the ram butting westward, northward, and southward, and no other beasts could stand before him, nor was there anyone to rescue from his power; but he did as he pleased and magnified himself. While I was observing, behold, a male goat was coming from the west over the surface of the whole earth without touching the ground; and the goat had a conspicuous horn between his eyes. And he came up to the ram that had the two horns, which I had seen standing in front of the canal, and rushed at him in his mighty wrath, and I saw him come beside the ram, and he was enraged at him; and he struck the ram and shattered his two horns, and the ram had no strength to withstand him. So he hurled him to the ground and trampled on him, and there was none to rescue the ram from his power. Then the male goat magnified himself exceedingly, but as soon as he was mighty, the large horn was broken; and in its place there came up four conspicuous horns toward the four winds of heaven. And out of them came forth a rather small horn which grew exceedingly great toward the south, toward the east, and toward the Beautiful Land. And it grew up to the host of heaven and caused some of the host and some of the stars to fall to the earth, and it trampled them down. It even magnified itself to be equal with the Commander of the host; and it removed the regular sacrifice from Him, and the place of His sanctuary was thrown down. And on account of transgression the host will be given over to the horn along with the regular sacrifice; and it will fling truth to the ground and perform its will and prosper. Then I heard a holy one speaking, and another holy one said to that particular one who was speaking, "How long will the vision about the regular sacrifice apply, while the transgression causes horror, so as to allow both the holy place and the host to be trampled?" And he said to me, "For 2,300 evenings and mornings; then the holy place will be properly restored."*

The vision projected Daniel into the future time when Medo-Persia would be the world power. In the vision Daniel saw himself in the fortress of the city of Susa beside the Ulai Canal. Susa was located approximately 230 miles east of Babylon and 120 miles north of the Persian Gulf.[2] After Medo-Persia became established as a great power, Susa was made the chief capital of the kingdom.[3] The city was situated between the Choaspes and Coprates Rivers.[4] Near the junction of the two rivers a fortress was built to protect the capital city.[5] A large canal connecting the two rivers and measuring approximately 900 feet wide was built to one side of the fortress. This canal was called Ulai.[6]

The vision portrayed a ram (male sheep) with two horns standing in front of the Ulai Canal. The ram represented Medo-Persia (v. 20). It corresponded to the arms and breast of silver of the image in chapter two and to the bear in chapter seven. The ram was an accurate representation of Medo-Persia, because in Bundehesch the guardian spirit of the Medo-Persian kingdom was portrayed in the form of a ram with sharp pointed horns, and the Persian king wore the head of a ram on his head when he stood at the head of his army.[7]

The two horns of the ram (representing Media and Persia) were long. The horn that rose later than the other became longer than the other. Media was a powerful kingdom before Persia became powerful; however, after they formed their partnership kingdom, Persia dominated Media. This was parallel to the bear which had one side higher than the other side (chpt. 7).

The ram butted toward the west, north and south, overpowering other animals at will and exalting itself. Coming from the east, Medo-Persia conquered primarily toward the west (Babylonia, Syria, Asia Minor), north (Armenia, regions around the Caspian Sea) and south (Egypt, Ethiopia).[8] Its massive army overwhelmed one kingdom after another until Medo-Persia became the largest kingdom up to that point in history.

The next thing Daniel saw was a male goat coming from the west. This goat represented Greece (v. 21). It corresponded to the brass belly and thighs of the image (chpt. 2) and the leopard with four wings (chpt. 7). Greece was situated west of Medo-Persia, and Alexander the Great moved his Greek-Macedonian army from that direction to attack the Medo-Persian kingdom.

The goat ran so rapidly over the surface of the earth that its feet did not touch the ground. This represented the tremendous speed with which Greece conquered the ancient world under Alexander's leadership (as noted with the four winged leopard — chpt. 7).

The goat had a great horn between its eyes. This horn symbolized the Grecian kingdom's first great king, Alexander the Great (v. 21). The number and location of the horn on this goat were unusual, for goats normally have two horns located above the eyes. As noted in chapter seven, eyes (when used symbolically) usually represent human intelligence. The fact that this one horn was located between the eyes of the goat would seem to imply that the symbolism was designed to represent a king with unique intelligence. Alexander the Great possessed unique intelligence. In spite of his youth (he was only twenty-two years old when he began to attack Medo-Persia), he amazed the ancient world with his military genius. Although he was opposed by much larger armies and greater financial resources than his own, his personal resourcefulness at devising successful tactics enabled him to crush the mighty Medo-Persian kingdom in about three years time (334-331 B.C.).[9]

The goat attacked the ram with such fury that it shattered the two horns of the ram, hurled the ram to the ground and trampled it under its feet. Under Alexander, Greece conquered the entire Medo-Persian kingdom, including both of its partners.

As soon as the goat became exceedingly powerful, the large horn between its eyes was broken. Four other horns rose up to replace it. Greece had hardly reached the peak of its power when Alexander the Great died at age thirty-two (323 B.C.). Four of his generals divided his kingdom among themselves. Ptolemy took Egypt, Cyrene, Cyprus, Palestine and several cities on the coast of Asia Minor. Seleucus possessed Syria, Babylonia, southern Asia Minor and the Iranian Plateau. Lysimachus controlled Thrace and western Asia Minor. Cassander ruled Macedonia and Greece proper.[10]

As Daniel watched the vision, a fifth little horn came out of one of the four horns on the goat. Although this horn was little at first, it grew to great influence toward the south, east and Beautiful Land. This indicated that a significant king would come to power in one of the four divisions of the Grecian kingdom (v. 23). This king was Antiochus IV, also known as Epiphanes, the eighth ruler of the Seleucid division.[11] Antiochus had a small beginning, for he was not the rightful heir to the throne, and he had to resort to bribery and flattery to become king. Once he became king, however, he began to make a significant impact through conquests and heavy-handed policies.[12] He attacked Egypt (south — 1 Maccabees 1:16-19) and Armenia and Elymais (east — 1 Macc. 3:31, 37; 6:1-4), and he tried to enforce new religious and civic policies upon the Jews in Palestine (the Beautiful Land).[13]

Daniel saw the little horn grow up to the starry host of heaven and cast down and trample some of the stars. In the Scriptures the Jews, particularly the righteous Jews, are sometimes symbolized by stars (Gen. 15:5; 22:17; Dan. 12:3; Rev. 12:1).[14] This indicated, then, that the king represented by the little horn would persecute and kill the Jews. Antiochus commanded the Jews to substitute pagan worship of idols for the worship of Jehovah. He ordered them to forget the Law, to profane their sabbaths and feast days, to stop circumcising infants, to offer the flesh of pigs and other unclean animals as sacrifices and to defile themselves with all kinds of perverted practices. He had copies of the Law torn and burned. He decreed that all Jews who kept copies of the Law, obeyed the Law or had children circumcised should be put to death. He had circumcised babies hanged. Through his cruel policies many righteous Jews were put to death (1 Macc. 1:29-64).

The little horn magnified itself to be equal with the Prince of the starry host. It removed the regular sacrifice of the Prince, harmed His sanctuary, threw truth to the ground and prospered in doing what it wanted to do. Inasmuch as the starry host represented Israel, the Prince of Israel would be God. Since God was the One who had instituted the Temple with its system of regular sacrifice, only He had the right to stop the sacrifice and to harm the Temple. Antiochus arrogantly entered the Temple of God in Jerusalem, stripped it of its sacred furniture and valuable ornaments, ordered the sacrifices ended there and the Temple polluted (1 Macc. 1:20-24, 41-50). Since this king did what only God had the right to do, he thereby magnified himself to be equal with the God of Israel. Antiochus threw the truth of God to the ground when he ordered the worship of Jehovah stopped and replaced with pagan Greek worship. He did enjoy success in the enforcement of his will for awhile. The reason he could prosper for awhile was the fact that God had a sovereign purpose for giving over the Jews and the regular sacrifice to him (v. 12).

Daniel heard one angel ask another how long the little horn would be able to carry on his horrible transgression against the people of Israel and the Temple. The other angel answered that this transgression would last for 2,300 days; then the Temple would be restored. Twenty-three hundred days is less than six and one-half years. Antiochus persecuted the Jews and desecrated the Temple from 171 to 165 B.C.[15] That span of time covered between six and seven years. Once Antiochus' influence in Israel was ended, the Jews did restore the Temple and its full worship service of Jehovah on December 25, 165 B.C.[16] That would place the starting point of the 2,300 days at September 6, 171 B.C.[17]

# THE INTERPRETATION
# OF THE VISION (8:15-26)

*And it came about when I, Daniel, had seen the vision that I sought to understand it; and behold, standing before me was one who looked like a man. And I heard the voice of a man between the banks of the Ulai, and he called out and said, "Gabriel, give this man an understanding of the vision." So he came near to where I was standing, and when he came I was frightened and fell on my face; but he said to me, "Son of man, understand that the vision pertains to the time of the end." Now while he was talking with me, I sank into a deep sleep with my face to the ground; but he touched me and made me stand upright. And he said, "Behold, I am going to let you know what will occur at the final period of the indignation; for it pertains to the appointed time of the end. The ram which you saw with the two horns represents the kings of Media and Persia. And the shaggy goat represents the kingdom of Greece, and the large horn that is between his eyes is the first king. And the broken horn and the four horns that arose in its place represent four kingdoms which will arise from his nation, although not with his power. And in the latter period of their rule, when the transgressors have run their course, a king will arise insolent and skilled in intrigue. And his power will be mighty, but not by his own power, and he will destroy to an extraordinary degree and prosper and perform his own will; he will destroy mighty men and the holy people. And through his shrewdness he will cause deceit to succeed by his influence; and he will magnify himself in his heart, and he will destroy many while they are at ease. He will even oppose the Prince of princes, but he will be broken without human agency. And the vision of the evenings and mornings which has been told is true; but keep the vision secret, for it pertains to many days in the future."*

While Daniel sought to understand the vision, the angel Gabriel appeared suddenly in the vision. Gabriel had the responsibility of carrying important messages from God to human beings on more than one occasion. He announced John the Baptist's birth to Zacharias and Jesus' birth to Mary (Lk. 1:19, 26). God instructed Gabriel to give Daniel understanding of the vision. As Gabriel approached Daniel to interpret the vision, Daniel became so terrified of this supernatural being that he fell to the ground on his face and eventually fainted. Gabriel revived Daniel and made him stand up.

Gabriel began the interpretation by declaring that the vision pertained to "the time of the end" (v. 17), "the appointed time of the end" (v. 19), and "the latter portion of the indignation" (v. 19).[18] It is apparent that "the time of the end" and "the latter portion of the indignation" are synonyms referring to the same period of time. But to what do they refer? A study of the term *indignation* throughout Scripture reveals that *the indignation* refers to the period of history during which God is indignant or angry with Israel because of its rebellion against Him. It is the time when God chastens Israel, usually at the hands of the Gentiles. *The indignation* included Israel's conquest and cruel treatment by Assyria (Isa. 10:5, 25) and Israel's conquest and captivity by Babylon (Lam. 2:6; Zech. 1:12), and it will continue through the end of the Tribulation Period (the end of Antichrist's rule at the second coming of Christ — Dan. 11:36). Thus, *the indignation* began during the 730's B.C. and will continue to the second coming of Christ. It is basically parallel to the times when the Gentiles are the predominant power in the world. It could be said that *The Indignation* is the title of God's program for Israel, and *The Times of The Gentiles* is the title of God's program for the Gentiles during the same basic period of history.

Gabriel said that Daniel's vision pertained to "the latter

# THE INDIGNATION AND THE TIMES OF THE GENTILES

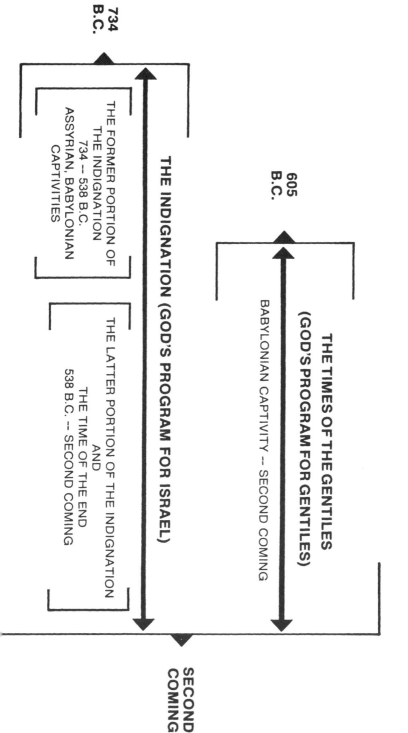

**734 B.C.**

THE INDIGNATION (GOD'S PROGRAM FOR ISRAEL)

THE FORMER PORTION OF THE INDIGNATION
734 -- 538 B.C.
ASSYRIAN, BABYLONIAN CAPTIVITIES

THE LATTER PORTION OF THE INDIGNATION
AND
THE TIME OF THE END
538 B.C. -- SECOND COMING

**605 B.C.**

THE TIMES OF THE GENTILES
(GOD'S PROGRAM FOR GENTILES)

BABYLONIAN CAPTIVITY -- SECOND COMING

SECOND COMING

portion of the indignation." The language implied that *the indignation* could be divided into two divisions: the former portion and the latter portion. It would appear that the former portion of *the indignation* included the Assyrian and Babylonian captivities of Israel (734 to 538 B.C.). The latter portion would stretch from the end of the Babylonian captivity to the second coming of Christ. Since "the latter portion of the indignation" and "the time of the end" are synonyms, "the time of the end" would also cover this same expanse of history.

Daniel received his vision during the former portion of *the indignation* (during the Babylonian captivity), but the rule of Medo-Persia and Greece and the fiendish policies of Antiochus Epiphanes were to take place during the latter portion of *the indignation* (after the Babylonian captivity). Through this vision, then, God revealed to Daniel that His indignation with Israel would continue for many future years.

It should be noted that Gabriel used the word "appointed" for the time of the end. This implied that God sovereignly determined the time of His indignation against Israel. God determined when Israel would be chastened and when that chastening would end.

Having made these introductory comments, Gabriel began to interpret the specific parts of the vision. He declared that the ram with two horns represented the Medo-Persian kingdom consisting of two partners. The goat symbolized the kingdom of Greece, and the large horn between its eyes stood for the first king of Greece (Alexander the Great). The four horns that replaced the broken horn on the head of the goat represented the four kingdoms which would result from the division of Alexander's kingdom after his untimely death. Gabriel declared that none of the rulers of those four kingdoms would rule with the same power as Alexander. Although some of those rulers were powerful, not one wielded the same power he did.

Concerning the little horn which came out of one of the four horns on the goat, Gabriel indicated that it represented a king. This king would arise from one of the four divisions of Alexander's kingdom. He would appear during the latter period of the rule of the four division kingdoms and when the transgressors would come to the full. As noted earlier, the little horn king was Antiochus Epiphanes. Antiochus came out of the Seleucid division (Syria, Babylonia, southern Asia Minor, Iranian Plateau) of Alexander's kingdom. He did appear during the latter portion of the rule of the four divisions, for he reigned from 175 to 164 B.C., and the four divisions fell to Rome in stages from 168 to 30 B.C.[19] The word "transgressors" referred to Jewish apostates, not to pagan Gentiles.[20] The little horn would appear when rebellious Jews would reach the peak of their falling away from God. Before Antiochus became king, both Greeks and Jews began to carry pagan Greek culture to Jerusalem and Israel. They gave themselves over to pleasure, questioned moral absolutes and undermined belief in the supernatural. Young and rich Jews, who were irritated by the restraints of the Law, gave themselves to this influence. They mocked the priests of God and the old pious Jews who worshiped Jehovah.[21] After Antiochus became king, some Jewish leaders, who were rebels against the Law of God, made a covenant with the Greeks. They built a pagan gymnasium in Jerusalem, forsook the covenant of God, practiced Greek customs, regarded themselves as Gentiles and worshiped Greek gods (1 Macc. 1:10-15, 43; 2 Macc. 4:7-17).

Gabriel declared that the little horn would be bold and crafty (v. 23).[22] Antiochus boldly took a throne that did not belong to him. He obtained rule through crafty measures. The little horn would possess great power, but not by himself (v. 24). Antiochus exhibited brutal power in his savage treatment of the Jews. It would appear that Satan empowered him supernaturally as a tool as Satan tried to annihilate the Jews to prevent the Messiah from coming. In conjunction with this, Gabriel said that the little horn would destroy to an extraordinary degree, including the destruction of mighty men and the holy people (v. 24). On one occasion Antiochus attacked Jerusalem, took a spoil of the city, burned major parts of it and tore down buildings and the city's walls (1 Macc. 1:29-31). On several occasions he slaughtered many Jews (1 Macc. 1:24, 37, 57-64; 2 Macc. 5:11-14, 23-26). The angel declared that the little horn would prosper and perform his will (v. 24). Antiochus enjoyed a considerable degree of success militarily and in his persecution of the Jews. To the righteous Jews it must have appeared that he was free to do as he pleased and was capable of prospering in evil indefinitely. As noted earlier, the only reason Antiochus could prosper in his abuse of the Jews was the fact that God had sovereignly turned over the Israelites to him as part of His indignation against Israel (vv. 12, 19).

Gabriel stated that the little horn through his own shrewdness would cause deceit to succeed (v. 25). Antiochus Epiphanes was noted for using cunningly devised deception to accomplish his goals. For example, in order to discover what his subjects thought of him, Antiochus would disguise himself and mingle among the people to hear their comments.[23] The little horn would consider himself to be great (v. 25). Antiochus thought so highly of himself that at times he "thought of establishing and requiring the worship of himself as a god."[24] As part of his cunning deceit, the little horn would destroy many when they felt safe and secure (v. 25). Antiochus sent a tax collector to Jerusalem with many soldiers. He had this man speak words of peace to the people of the city in order to deceive them into a sense of security.

Once the people let down their guard, Antiochus' man attacked Jerusalem savagely. The city was plundered; large parts were burned or torn down; many Jews were killed, and women and children were carried into slavery (1 Macc. 1:29-33).

According to Gabriel, the little horn would even stand against the Prince of princes (v. 25). Antiochus did stand against the Most High God. He plundered and defiled God's Temple, had that Temple rededicated as a worship place of Zeus (the chief Greek god), had a pagan altar built over the altar of God and commanded that the regular sacrifices be replaced by the sacrifice of pigs.[25] He even went so far as to have coins minted with the following inscription: "Antiochus Theos Epiphanes — the God Made Manifest."[26]

The little horn would not be allowed to carry on his bold activities indefinitely. Gabriel declared that he would be broken without human agency (v. 25). This meant that no human beings would put him to death. Acording to 1 Maccabees 6:1-16, Antiochus died from great grief in the city of Babylon as the result of military reversals in Persia and Palestine. Other ancient reports indicated that he died in Persia of epilepsy, madness or disease.[27] Although these accounts differ on the cause of death, they all indicate that Antiochus died apart from human agency. God's judgment caught up with this persecutor of His people.

At the    conclusion of the interpretation, Gabriel emphasized the fact that the vision concerning the 2,300 days (evenings and mornings — compare v. 14) of Israel's persecution by Antiochus was true. In other words, it portrayed what actually would happen. Daniel needed this assertion, for it would be difficult for him to believe that Israel would be chastened for many more years.

Gabriel commanded Daniel to preserve the vision (v. 26). The word translated "secret" does not mean to hide. God does not give revelation to be hidden. Instead, it means to *shut up* or *preserve.*[28] Daniel was to record this vision in permanent, written form, so that it could be preserved for future generations. The reason for the preservation of the vision was this: the vision dealt with future events that would not be fulfilled for many days. Indeed, the part of the vision that dealt with Antiochus' abuse of Israel did not begin to be fulfilled until 380 years after Daniel received the vision. It wouldn't be until then that this prophetic vision would make its greatest impact upon people.

## DANIEL'S REACTION
## TO THE VISION (8:27)

*Then I, Daniel, was exhausted and sick for days. Then I got up again and carried on the king's business; but I was astounded at the vision, and there was none to explain it.*

Daniel was so emotionally distraught by this vision that he fainted and was sick in bed for several days. After he regained strength, he returned to his duties in the service of the king, but he continued to be astonished by the vision. Even though Gabriel had interpreted the vision for him, Daniel did not understand it fully. Evidently his mind continued to be perplexed by it for a long time.

# A CONCLUDING NOTATION

It is important to note that the little horns of chapters seven and eight are two distinct persons. Several factors make this distinction clear:

| Little Horn of Chapter Seven | Little Horn of Chapter Eight |
|---|---|
| 1. Would come from Rome (fourth kingdom). | 1. Would come from Greece (third kingdom). |
| 2. Would be an eleventh horn, rooting up three of ten horns. | 2. Would be a fifth horn, coming out of one of four horns. |
| 3. Would persecute God's people for 42 months or 3½ years. | 3. Would persecute God's people for 2,300 days or over 6 years. |

The little horn of chapter seven is Antichrist; the little horn of chapter eight is Antiochus Epiphanes. From the perspective of Daniel's day, the little horn of chapter seven would live in the far distant future, but the little horn of chapter eight would live in the more immediate future.

Although the two little horns would be two distinct persons living in different periods of history, they would be characterized by similar attitudes and actions. Both would oppose God, magnify themselves to the level of deity and persecute the people of God. In other words, both would be extreme expressions of fallen man's mania to rule the world apart from God.

# THE TIMES OF THE GENTILES

| IMAGE -- CHPT. 2 | BEASTS -- CHPT. 7 | BEASTS -- CHPT. 8 | KINGDOMS REPRESENTED |
|---|---|---|---|
| HEAD OF GOLD | WINGED LION | | BABYLON |
| ARMS AND BREAST OF SILVER | BEAR | RAM WITH TWO HORNS | MEDO-PERSIA |
| BELLY AND THIGHS OF BRONZE | WINGED, FOUR-HEADED LEOPARD | MALE GOAT WITH ONE GREAT HORN, FOUR HORNS AND LITTLE HORN | GREECE |
| LEGS OF IRON, FEET AND TOES OF IRON AND CLAY | NONDESCRIPT BEAST WITH TEN HORNS AND LITTLE HORN | | ROME |
| STONE THAT BECOMES A GREAT MOUNTAIN | MESSIAH AND SAINTS GIVEN A KINGDOM | | KINGDOM OF GOD |

# GOD'S EXTENDED FUTURE PROGRAM FOR ISRAEL

## A SIGNIFICANT OBSERVATION

Chapter nine contains one of the most significant prophecies in all the Old Testament Scriptures. It foretold the precise time when Messiah would be present in the world. As a result, that prophecy is one of the strongest biblical evidences to the effect that Jesus of Nazareth is the Messiah whom God promised to Israel throughout its Old Testament history.

## DANIEL'S INQUISITIVE RESEARCH (9:1-2)

> *In the first year of Darius the son of Ahasuerus, of Median descent, who was made king over the kingdom of the Chaldeans — in the first year of his reign I, Daniel, observed in the books the number of the years which was revealed as the word of the Lord to Jeremiah the prophet for the completion of the desolations of Jerusalem, namely, seventy years.*

During the first year of the reign of Darius (the Darius or Gubaru of chpts. 5 and 6), Daniel found some interesting information as he read the sacred books of the Jews that had been written thus far. He found that God had declared through the prophet, Jeremiah, that the Babylonian captivity of the Jews would last for seventy years (Jer. 25:11-12; 29:10-14). This information was of special interest to Daniel because of the year in which he read it — 538 B.C. [1] Since the captivity had begun in 605 B.C., it was now nearing its designated conclusion.

# DANIEL'S PENITENT PRAYER (9:3-19)

*So I gave my attention to the Lord God to seek Him by prayer and supplications, with fasting, sackcloth, and ashes. And I prayed to the Lord my God and confessed and said, "Alas, O Lord, the great and awesome God, who keeps His covenant and lovingkindness for those who love Him and keep His commandments, we have sinned, committed iniquity, acted wickedly, and rebelled, even turning aside from Thy commandments and ordinances. Moreover, we have not listened to Thy servants the prophets, who spoke in Thy name to our kings, our princes, our fathers, and all the people of the land. Righteousness belongs to Thee, O Lord, but to us open shame, as it is in this day — to the men of Judah, the inhabitants of Jerusalem, and all Israel, those who are near by and those who are far away in all the countries to which Thou hast driven them, because of their unfaithful deeds which they have committed against Thee. Open shame belongs to us, O Lord, to our kings, our princes, and our fathers, because we have sinned against Thee. To the Lord our God belong compassion and forgiveness, for we have rebelled against Him; nor have we obeyed the voice of the Lord our God, to walk in His teachings which He set before us through His servants the prophets. Indeed all Israel has transgressed Thy law and turned aside, not obeying Thy voice; so the curse has been poured out on us, along with the oath which is written in the law of Moses the servant of God, for we have sinned against Him. Thus He has confirmed His words which He had spoken against us and against our rulers who ruled us, to bring on us great calamity; for under the whole heaven there has not been done anything like what was done to Jerusalem. As it is written in the law of Moses, all this calamity has come on us; yet we have not sought the favor of the Lord our God by turning from our iniquity and giving attention to Thy truth. Therefore, the Lord has kept the calamity in store and brought it on us; for the Lord our God is righteous with respect to all His deeds which He has done, but we have not obeyed His voice. And now, O Lord our God, who hast brought Thy people out of the land of Egypt with a mighty hand and hast made a name for Thyself, as it is this day — we have sinned, we have been wicked. O Lord, in accordance with all Thy righteous acts, let now Thine anger and Thy wrath turn away from Thy city Jerusalem, Thy holy mountain; for because of our sins and the iniquities of our fathers, Jerusalem and Thy people have become a reproach to all those around us. So now, our God, listen to the prayer of Thy servant and to his*

*supplications, and for Thy sake, O Lord, let Thy face shine on*
*Thy desolate sanctuary. O my God, incline Thine ear and hear!*
*Open Thine eyes and see our desolations and the city which is*
*called by Thy name; for we are not presenting our supplications*
*before Thee on account of any merits of our own, but on account*
*of Thy great compassion. O Lord, hear! O Lord, listen and take*
*action! For Thine own sake, O my God, do not delay, because*
*Thy city and Thy people are called by Thy name."*

Daniel deliberately began to approach God with an
attitude and prayer of genuine repentance. His attitude was
indicated by two things. First, he approached God as
Adonai (Lord, Master — v. 3).[2] He recognized the sovereign
Lordship of God over Israel and its captivity. Second, he
exhibited the outward manifestations of repentance in his
day: fasting and the wearing of sackcloth and ashes.

Daniel's prayer consisted of two major parts. The first
part contained confession (vv. 4-15). Daniel emphasized the
greatness and faithfulness of God. Because He is so great,
He should be feared by Israel. Because He faithfully keeps
His covenants and shows lovingkindness, there was hope for
Israel, if it would repent and love and obey God (v. 4).

Daniel hid nothing concerning the evils of Israel which
had caused its captivity. He honestly confessed that the
nation had missed the mark, acted perversely, done known
wrong and rebelled against God's authority.[3] All this had
been caused by the nation's departure from the Word of
God. In addition the nation's leaders, the earlier generations
and the people in general had refused to listen to the
prophets whom God had sent to rebuke the people and warn
of impending judgment if they would not repent.

Daniel made it clear that God was not to blame for Israel's
shame. God had acted righteously. It was all the Jews, no
matter where they were now located or what their status in
life, who were to blame. All had rebelled. God had given
Israel plenty of warning concerning the curse of judgment
He had vowed to bring upon the nation if it were to rebel

persistently. As far back as Moses, He had issued the warning. But Israel did not repent and return to God's Word. For that reason through the centuries God watched over His vowed curse of judgment, keeping it in a constant state of readiness to be administered at the right time.[4]

Daniel reminded God that in the past He had made a great name for Himself before the world by miraculously delivering the people of Israel from their bondage in Egypt. Daniel did this because he was about to ask God to do a similar thing again for Israel and thereby increase the greatness of His name.

The second part of Daniel's prayer consisted of supplication (vv. 16-19). He pled with God to forgive Israel and to restore the people, the city of Jerusalem and the Temple to their former estate. Jerusalem and the Temple had been destroyed by the Babylonians in 586 B.C. They had remained desolate ever since. Daniel stated that this judgment of Israel, Jerusalem and the Temple had dishonored the name of God among the pagan Gentiles. It seemed to these pagans that the gods of Babylon were more powerful than Israel's God. For that reason Daniel petitioned God to act with favor toward Israel, Jerusalem and the Temple, not because the Jews deserved it, but because God is very merciful, and His reputation was at stake.

Daniel concluded his prayer by vigorously assailing the throne of God with a bombardment of requests. He asked God to hear, forgive, listen and act. Finally, he begged God not to delay His favorable action on behalf of the people and city that were called by His name.

This last request gives a clue concerning why Daniel prayed such an intense prayer of repentance at this time. In one of the Jeremiah passages (29:10-14) which Daniel had read, God had declared that He would end the captivity in conjunction with Israel calling upon, praying to and searching for God with all its heart. Knowing that the designated conclusion of the captivity was near, Daniel feared that God might delay the conclusion if the Jews didn't call upon Him with prayers of repentance. In order to prevent such a delay, Daniel began to do the very thing that would bring an end to the captivity.

## GOD'S REACTION TO
## DANIEL'S PRAYER (9:20-27)

*Now while I was speaking and praying, and confessing my sin and the sin of my people Israel, and presenting my supplication before the Lord my God in behalf of the holy mountain of my God, while I was still speaking in prayer, then the man Gabriel, whom I had seen in the vision previously, came to me in my extreme weariness about the time of the evening offering. And he gave me instruction and talked with me, and said, "O Daniel, I have now come forth to give you insight with understanding. At the beginning of your supplications the command was issued, and I have come to tell you, for you are highly esteemed; so give heed to the message and gain understanding of the vision. Seventy weeks have been decreed for your people and your holy city, to finish the transgression, to make an end of sin, to make atonement for iniquity, to bring in everlasting righteousness, to seal up vision and prophecy, and to anoint the most holy place. So you are to know and discern that from the issuing of a decree to restore and rebuild Jerusalem until Messiah the Prince there will be seven weeks and sixty-two weeks; it will be built again, with plaza and moat, even in times of distress. Then after the sixty-two weeks the Messiah will be cut off and have nothing, and the people of the prince who is to come will destroy the city and the sanctuary. And its end will come with a flood; even to the end there will be war; desolations are determined. And he will make a firm covenant with the many for one week, but in the middle of the week he will put a stop to sacrifice and grain offering; and on the wing of abominations will come one who makes desolate, even until a complete destruction, one that is decreed, is poured out on the one who makes desolate."*

Before Daniel finished praying God sent the angel, Gabriel, in the form of a man to interrupt him. Gabriel reached Daniel about the time of the evening offering (about 3 to 4 p.m.).[5] God had sent Gabriel for the purpose of making Daniel wise with understanding concerning the vision of chapter eight. Although Daniel had received that vision thirteen years earlier, he continued to be wearied by confusion concerning it. What confused Daniel was this: if the Babylonian captivity of the Jews was to last for seventy years, and if those seventy years were near their end, then why in the vision of chapter eight had God pictured a further chastening of Israel for many years into the future? It would appear that the vision had caused Daniel to fear that God might delay the end of the captivity. It was that fear that drove Daniel to be so intense in his prayer of repentance.

Gabriel was to end Daniel's confusion by delivering new revelation from God. It is significant that Gabriel was chosen to deliver this new revelation, since he was the angel involved with the vision that caused the confusion. The new revelation would indicate that, although God would end the present Babylonian captivity very soon, He would continue to chasten His people of Israel for an extended period of time into the future. The captivity was only the first portion of God's indignation against Israel; the latter portion of the indignation would come after the captivity. This would indicate that God was in sovereign control of Israel's destiny.

The reason God saw fit to send Gabriel with this revelation was the fact that Daniel was highly esteemed by God. The word translated "esteemed" literally means *precious*.[6] Daniel was given this special privilege because he was very precious to God. This expression is a great commentary on the grace of God and the godly character and life of Daniel.

Gabriel exhorted Daniel to give close attention to the revelation, because it would give him understanding of the vision in chapter eight.

The new revelation is contained in verses twenty-four through twenty-seven. In this passage God indicated that He would continue to chasten Israel for at least seventy more sevens of years beyond the end of the Babylonian captivity. As noted earlier, this passage contains the only Old Testament prophecy presenting the exact time of Messiah's presentation to Israel in His first coming. It was fitting that Gabriel delivered this prophecy about Messiah's first coming, for several centuries later he would deliver the revelation concerning Messiah's conception and birth to Mary (Lk. 1:26-38).

If the new revelation is to be understood properly, several significant things concerning it must be noted. First (v. 24), this prophecy concerns Daniel's people and holy city; therefore, the prophecy must be applied completely to Israel and Jerusalem.

Second (v. 24), the amount of time covered by the prophecy is 490 years. Gabriel said that seventy weeks (literally, *seventy sevens*) had been decreed by God for Israel and Jerusalem. Seventy sevens is the same as seventy times seven or 490. God had decreed 490 units of time. But how much time would be involved in these 490 units? Did God decree 490 years, 490 days, 490 weeks or 490 months? It had to be 490 years, for that is the only length of time that would work historically. According to this prophecy, Messiah would be present in Israel before the 490 time units would end. As will be seen later, the 490 time units began in 445 B.C. It is a historic fact that Messiah was not present in Israel within 490 days (about one and one-third years), 490 weeks (about nine and one-half years) or 490 months (about 41 years) after 445 B.C. In addition, seventy sevens of years would have been very meaningful to the Jews. God had divided their calendar into seven year periods with every seventh year being a sabbatic year (Lev. 25:3-9), and their Babylonian captivity was to last seventy years because they had violated seventy sabbatic years over the course of 490 years (2 Chr. 36:21). Daniel himself had been thinking in terms of years in the context of this prophecy (9:1-2).

Third (v. 24), the 490 years of the prophecy would be necessary to accomplish six things with regard to Israel and Jerusalem:

1. "to finish the transgression." The word translated "transgression" has the root meaning *to rebel.*[7] With the word "the" in this context, it refers to the Jews' specific sin of rebellion against the rule of God. This rebellion was the root sin which prompted all of Israel's other sins. Gabriel was saying that Israel would not stop its rebellion against God's rule until these 490 years would run their course. In agreement with this, other Scriptures indicate that Israel will not repent, turn to God and be saved until the second coming of Christ at the end of these 490 years (Zech. 12:10-13:1; Rom. 11:25-27).

2. "to make an end of sin." The word translated "sin" is plural, referring to *the actual sins of daily life.*[8] These 490 years would run their course before Israel would end its sins of daily life. Since these sins are prompted by the sin of rebellion against God's rule, they will not end until that root sin is finished at Christ's second coming.

3. "to make atonement for iniquity." Jesus Christ atoned Israel's perverse sins when He died on the cross, but that atonement will not actually be applied to Israel until the nation personally appropriates it by accepting Jesus as its Messiah and Savior. Israel will not do that until Christ's second coming at the end of the 490 years.

4. "to bring in everlasting righteousness." On the one hand, this could refer to the righteousness that will be brought to Israel at the end of the 490 years. In the past, as the result of periodic revivals, Israel had experienced righteousness. However, that righteousness was temporary, for eventually the nation rebelled against God again. But

when Israel repents and believes in Jesus Christ at His second coming, it will never rebel against God again (Jer. 31:31-34; Ezek. 36:22-32). It will be given righteousness that will last forever. On the other hand, the literal translation of this phrase (*to bring in righteousness of ages*[9]) may indicate that this refers to the righteous rule that Messiah will establish on earth in conjunction with His second coming at the end of the 490 years (Isa. 11:1-5; Jer. 23:5-6; 33:15-18). This rule will be characterized by the righteousness that has been characteristic of God throughout the ages. The bringing in of the future rule of righteousness on earth has been the goal of the ages of history ever since that rule was lost on earth through man's rebellion in Eden against God's sovereignty. In other words, this may refer to the future, earthly Kingdom of God portrayed in the dreams of chapters two and seven and that will last forever.

5. "to seal up vision and prophecy." The thrust of this phrase seems to be as follows: revelation that comes through vision or prophecy no longer has to be of concern to people once that revelation has been fulfilled. The vision or prophecy can be sealed up in the sense of being laid aside from the realm of active concern. The word translated "to seal up" is the same word which was translated "to make an end" in the phrase "to make an end of sins" earlier in this verse.[10] It would appear that there is an intended relationship between the two phrases. That relationship is as follows: when Israel will make an end of its daily sins at the end of the 490 years, then all revelation that came through vision and prophecy concerning God's chastening of Israel can be sealed up. The people of Israel will no longer have to be concerned about that revelation, for all the foretold chastening will have been fulfilled. Since their sins which caused chastening will have ended, there will be no further need for chastening.

6. "to anoint the most holy place." A literal translation of

this phrase is as follows: *to anoint a holy of holies.*[11] In
biblical times, anointing had the significance of consecration for service (Ex. 28:41; 29:36; 40:9-15). When the
expression *holy of holies* was used without the word *the*, as
it is here, it usually referred to the holy articles of the
Tabernacle or Temple (Ex. 29:37) or to the whole Temple
complex area (Ezek. 43:12).[12] In light of these factors and
the context of chapter nine, it would appear that Gabriel
was saying the following: when Messiah will come in His
second coming at the end of the 490 years, the Temple
complex area in Jerusalem will be anointed in consecration
for God's service. The Scriptures indicate that the Temple
will be rebuilt for the service of God during the Millennial
reign of Messiah on earth (Ezek. 40-48). Thus, the Temple
area will be anointed in preparation for the rebuilding of
that Millennial Temple. It is interesting to note that the
Ezekiel 43:12 passage referred to above is part of the Ezekiel
passage concerning the Millennial Temple and refers to this
future anointing of the Temple area.

The fourth significant thing to note concerning the new
revelation to Daniel is the starting point of the 490 years (v.
25). Gabriel indicated that the starting point would be the
issuing of a decree to restore and rebuild Jerusalem with
plaza and moat. At first glance this statement poses a
problem, for Medo-Persian kings issued several different
decrees permitting the rebuilding of various parts of
Jerusalem. The first decree was issued by Cyrus in 538 or 537
B.C.; the second was by Darius in 519 B.C.; the third was
by Artaxerxes in 458 B.C.; and the fourth was by
Artaxerxes in 445 B.C.[13] The major issue, then, is this: to
which of these decrees was Gabriel referring in Daniel 9:25?

Before this question can be answered, two things must be
noted concerning the decree of Daniel 9:25. First, that
decree would permit the rebuilding of plaza and moat. The
word *plaza* refers to the broad open space just inside a city's

gates — the space that was the center of city life.[14] It should be noted that this was space inside of *gates* (2 Chr. 32:6). But a city does not have gates unless it has a wall. Thus, the construction of a plaza necessitated the construction of a city wall. The word *moat* refers to a trench or ditch designed for the defense of a city.[15] It was the common practice of walled cities to dig deep trenches around their walls as part of their defenses.[16] Thus, the building of a moat implies the construction of a wall and the construction of defenses. When the terms *plaza* and *moat* are joined together, they indicate the building of a city's defenses (including a wall with gates and a moat). In light of this, it can be concluded that the decree of Daniel 9:25 permitted the rebuilding of Jerusalem's defenses (including the rebuilding of its wall and moat).

The second thing to be noted about the decree of Daniel 9:25 is this: its time of issue would be the starting point of a period of sixty-nine sevens of years (sixty-nine times seven or 483 years) that would end when Messiah would be present in the world in His first coming.

These two factors concerning the decree of Daniel 9:25 provide two tests which can be applied to the four Medo-Persian decrees mentioned above. The application of these two tests will indicate which Medo-Persian decree was the one to which Gabriel referred.

The first test is this: which decree permitted the rebuilding of Jerusalem's defenses including its wall and moat? The decrees by Cyrus (538 or 537 B.C.), Darius (519 B.C.) and Artaxerxes (458 B.C.) fail this test. It is a fact of history that the defenses of Jerusalem were not rebuilt as the result of any of these three decrees. As late as 445 B.C. Nehemiah received word that the walls of Jerusalem were still broken down (Neh. 1; 2). In addition, an event that took place several years after these three decrees were issued indicates conclusively that none of these decrees permitted the rebuilding of Jerusalem's walls. Sometime after Artaxerxes' decree in 458 B.C., the Jews in Palestine began to rebuild the walls of Jerusalem on their own initiative.[17] They did not complete the work, however, for their enemies wrote a letter to King Artaxerxes (Ezra 4:8-16). This letter warned the king that, if the Jews rebuilt Jerusalem's walls, they would rebel against him. In response to this letter, Artaxerxes decreed that the Jews stop their rebuilding activity. No further rebuilding could be done until the king would issue a future decree permitting it. (It should be noted that Artaxerxes left a loophole for a later decree to be issued that would permit the rebuilding of the walls. God's sovereign hand was at work in the wording of the negative decree [Ezra 4:17-22].) This negative decree of Artaxerxes is most significant in relationship to the three earlier decrees mentioned above. As noted in chapter six, it was the nature of Medo-Persian law that no king could reverse an earlier decree made by himself or one of his royal predecessors (Dan. 6:8, 12, 15; Est. 1:19; 8:8). In light of this, if any of the three earlier decrees had permitted the Jews to rebuild Jerusalem's walls, then Artaxerxes could not have issued this later decree forbidding the rebuilding of the walls. The fact that he did issue such a decree is conclusive evidence that the three earlier decrees did not permit the rebuilding of Jerusalem's walls. Thus, the decree of Daniel 9:25 was not the decree of Cyrus (538 or 537 B.C.), of Darius (519 B.C.) or of Artaxerxes (458 B.C.). Instead, it had to be the decree of Artaxerxes issued to Nehemiah in 445 B.C. (Neh. 1; 2).

The second test to be applied to the four Medo-Persian decrees is this: which decree could be the starting point of the 483 years that would end when Messiah would be present in the world in His first coming? The decrees of Cyrus and Darius fail this test. Using the Cyrus decree as the starting point (538 or 537 B.C.), the 483 years would end approximately fifty years before Jesus, the Messiah, was born. Using the Darius decree (519 B.C.), the 483 years would end more than thirty years before Jesus' birth. Thus, both of these decrees were issued too early to be the decree of Daniel 9:25. Both of Artazerxes' decrees (458 and 445 B.C.) could pass this test, but the first of these (458 B.C.) must be disqualified, because it failed the first test.

The only decree that passes both tests is the decree of Artaxerxes to Nehemiah in 445 B.C. Therefore, the starting point to the 490 years of the prophecy in Daniel 9 was March, 445 B.C. (Neh. 2:1-8).

The fifth significant thing to note concerning the prophecy in Daniel 9 is this: the time when Messiah would be present in His first coming (v. 25). Gabriel said that the time from the issuing of the decree until Messiah the Prince would be sixty-nine sevens of years (sixty-nine times seven equals 483 years). In other words, 483 years after 445 B.C. Messiah would be present in the world. (Gabriel divided the sixty-nine sevens of years into two periods: seven sevens [49 years] amd sixty-two sevens [434 years]. Many scholars are convinced that he did this to indicate that it would take forty-nine years after the decree in 445 B.C. to complete the rebuilding of Jerusalem.[18] It took that long because the Jews met much opposition to their rebuilding activity [Neh. 4; 6:1-7:4]. Thus, the city and its defenses were rebuilt in times of distress just as was foretold by Gabriel.)

When during the lifetim of Jesus, the messiah, did the 483 years end? When computing the data provided by Gabriel, one must keep in mind that in ancient tims a year was reckoned to consist of 360 days.[19] The ancient peoples of India, Persia, Babylon, Egypt, Greece, Italy, Central America and China had a calendar system with a 360-day year.[20] The Bible followed that ancient system (Gen. 7:11, 24; 8:4 — five months contained 150 days; Rev. 11:2-3; 12:6, 14; 13:5 — forty-two months or three and one-half years contained 1,260 days.) Thus, the 483 years between Ar-

taxerxes' decree and the designated time in Messiah's life
would amount to 173,880 days (483 years times 360 days).
According to Gabriel, starting with Artaxerxes' decree in
March, 445 B.C., the addition of 173,880 days would bring
one to the exact time when something significant would
happen in Messiah's life on earth. Research led Sir Robert
Anderson to conclude that Artaxerxes issued his decree to
Nehemiah on March 14, 445 B.C.[21] Beginning with that
date, the 173,880 days end on April 6, 32 A.D.[22] Thus, the
483 years ended on April 6, 32 A.D.

What significant thing happened to Jesus, the Messiah,
on April 6, 32 A.D.? When referring to the end of the first
483 years, Gabriel said: "until Messiah the Prince."
Whatever happened to Jesus on April 6, 32 A.D., it must
have been related significantly to His being the Prince, the
King of Israel. Sir Robert Anderson concluded that April 6,
32 A.D., was the day on which Jesus officially presented
Himself as Messiah to Israel through His triumphal entry
into Jerusalem on the foal of a donkey.[23] Zechariah 9:9 had
declared that Israel could identify its King in the following
manner: He would come to Jerusalem mounted on the foal
of a donkey. Some of the crowd on that Palm Sunday
recognized the significance of Jesus' actions on that day, for
they called Him King (Lk. 19:37-38). As Jesus approached
Jerusalem on that day, He wept over the city and said: "If
you had known in this day, even you, the things which make
for peace! But now they have been hidden from your eyes."
He warned Jerusalem that it would suffer great disaster
"because you did not recognize the time of your visitation"
(Lk. 19:41-44). Jesus' language indicated that that particular
day had been marked out by God as the time of Jerusalem's
visitation by her Messiah Prince — the day which could
have brought lasting peace to that city if its people had
accepted Jesus for who He was. It also indicated that the
Jews should have recognized that that particular day (April

6, 32 A.D.) was the day on which Messiah would visit Jerusalem as Prince. Why should they have recognized this? Because several centuries earlier in Daniel 9:25, God had revealed the exact time when Messiah would present Himself as Prince to Israel.

The sixth significant thing to note about the Daniel 9 prophecy is this: after the first 483 years of the prophecy would be completed, Messiah would be "cut off and have nothing" (v. 26). The word translated "cut off" was used for the death penalty (Lev. 7:20, 21, 25, 27) and often referred to a violent death (1 Sam. 17:51; Obad. 9; Nah. 3:15).[24] In this instance it referred to the fact that Messiah would be condemned to suffer the death penalty — a violent death by crucifixion. The expression, "and have nothing" meant that, when Messiah would die, He would not have all that should properly belong to the Messiah.[25] As Messiah, He should have had a royal crown of gold and precious jewels, but He had a crown of thorns (Mt. 27:29). He should have had a royal robe, but He was stripped of His clothing (Jn. 19:23-24). He should have had a royal throne, but He was given the cross (Jn. 19:17-18). He should have had the reception and acclaim of His people, but He received their rejection (Jn. 19:14-15 and scorn (Mt. 27:39-44).

Gabriel said that Messiah would be cut off *after* the first 483 years. As noted earlier, the 483 years ended on Palm Sunday, 32 A.D. It is a fact of history that Jesus was crucified several days *after* His triumphal entry on Palm Sunday (Mk. 11-15). Since the triumphal entry took place on April 6, 32 A.D., and the crucifixion transpired several days later, then the crucifixion also took place in the spring of 32 A.D. The chronology of Daniel 9 indicated that the triumphal entry would take place then, but does the chronology of the New Testament indicate that the triumphal entry and crucifixion took place in the spring of 32 A.D.?

Several chronological factors in the New Testament play a role in determining the year of Christ's triumphal entry and death. Two of these factors will be examined here.[26] First, Luke declared that John the Baptist began his ministry in the fifteenth year of the reign of Tiberius Caesar (Lk. 3:1-3). There is substantial evidence to the effect that Tiberius began his reign in 14 A.D.; therefore, the fifteenth year of Tiberius' reign would have been in 28 A.D.[27] Statements made by John near the beginning of his ministry seem to indicate that he began that ministry in the spring.[28] Thus, John began his ministry in the spring, 28 A.D. Since John had an established ministry before Christ came to him (Mk. 1:5-9), it is probable that Christ was baptized and began His ministry late in the fall season.[29] This would mean, then, that Christ began His ministry in the fall of 28 A.D. Epiphanius, a church bishop on Cyprus during the fourth and fifth centuries, declared that Christ was baptized in November of 28 A.D.[30] There is substantial evidence for concluding that Jesus ministered for three years plus several months.[31] Beginning with late fall, 28 A.D., an additional three years plus several months would end in the spring of 32 A.D. Thus, this first New Testament chronological factor does indicate that Christ's triumphal entry and crucifixion took place in the spring of 32 A.D. In the fourth century Bishop Epiphanius stated that Christ died in the spring of 32 A.D.[32]

Second, during the first Passover of Jesus' ministry, He cleansed Herod's Temple in Jerusalem (Jn. 2:11-16).[33] On that occasion the Jews said: "It took forty-six years to build this temple" (Jn. 2:20). Many historians agree that Herod's Temple was not finally completed until 64 A.D.[34] In light of this, the Jews' statement meant that Herod's Temple was in the forty-sixth year of its building at the time of their statement — also at the time of the first Passover of Jesus' ministry. Research has led several historians to conclude

that Herod began actual building of the Temple in 18
B.C.[35] Beginning with 18 B.C., forty-six years would bring
one to 29 A.D. (there is only one year from 1 B.C. to 1
A.D.). Thus, the first Passover of Jesus' ministry was in the
spring of 29 A.D. Jesus' ministry covered four Passovers.[36]
Beginning with the first Passover in 29 A.D., the fourth
Passover would have been in the spring of 32 A.D. Since
Jesus was crucified in conjunction with the last Passover of
His ministry, this would mean that Christ made His
triumphal entry and died in the spring of 32 A.D.

New Testament chronology does agree with the
chronology of the Daniel 9 prophecy. It thereby confirms
the accuracy of that prophecy and demonstrates conclusively that Jesus of Nazareth is the Messiah spoken of by
Gabriel in Daniel 9:25-26.

The seventh significant thing to note about the Daniel 9
prophecy is as follows: Jerusalem and the Temple would be
destroyed after the first 483 years of the prophecy would be
completed (v. 26). Since the 483 years ended in 32 A.D.,
this meant that the city and Temple would be destroyed
sometime after 32 A.D. — after Messiah would be rejected
by Israel and crucified. Thus, although Gabriel had just
foretold the rebuilding of Jerusalem and the Temple after
the Babylonian captivity (surely to Daniel's encouragement), he now foretold another destruction of them
centuries after the rebuilding (surely to Daniel's discourage-
ment). This would confirm the fact that God's chastening of
Israel would not cease with the end of the Babylonian
captivity, and it would help Daniel understand why the
vision in chapter eight portrayed more suffering for Israel
for centuries to come.

The fact that Jerusalem and the Temple would be
destroyed after Messiah would be cut off indicated that this
future destruction would be God's sovereign judgment upon
Israel for rejecting Messiah in His first coming. As noted

earlier, Jesus warned Jerusalem about its destruction that
would come because it did not recognize the time of its
visitation by Messiah (Lk. 19:41-44).

Gabriel said that Jerusalem and the Temple would be
destroyed by a certain people. It is a fact that the city and
Temple were destroyed by the Romans in 70 A.D., some
thirty-eight years after 32 A.D. Thus, the Romans are the
people to whom Gabriel referred. From today's perspective,
it can be understood that this meant that this destruction
would come while the fourth kingdom of Gentile world rule
(the Roman Empire represented by the legs of iron in
chapter two and the nondescript beast in chapter seven)
would be dominating the world.

Gabriel declared that the Roman people would belong to
a coming prince (literally, *a prince the one coming*).[37] Thus,
this coming prince would be a Roman ruler (this prince
cannot be Messiah the Prince referred to in v. 25, for the
Romans who destroyed Jerusalem did not belong to
Messiah, and Messiah is not a Roman prince).[38] The literal
translation *a prince the one coming* indicated that this ruler
and his coming were already known to Daniel. Daniel had
already been informed that such a one would come in the
future to destroy the people of God.[39] Indeed, this coming
prince would be the little horn or Antichrist who had been
revealed to Daniel in chapter seven some fifteen years
earlier.[40] As noted in that chapter, Antichrist would be the
last great ruler of the Revived Roman Empire immediately
before the second coming of Messiah.

The next thing Gabriel said was this: "And its end will
come with a flood; even to the end there will be war;
desolations are determined." The word translated "flood" is
used in Nahum 1:8 for the outpouring of God's wrath.[41]
Some refer the word "its" back to "the city," saying "its end"
is referring to the destruction of Jerusalem, but this is
grammatically incorrect.[42] Instead, "its" refers back to the

coming prince, Antichrist, and should be translated *his*.[43] Thus, Gabriel was saying that Antichrist's end would come with an outpouring of God's wrath. That such would be the case was seen earlier in chapter seven. As noted in that chapter, Antichrist will wage war against God and God's people until his judgment at the second coming of Christ. Because such would be the case, Gabriel said that there would be war "even to the end" — the end of the 490 years of the Daniel 9 prophecy. This meant that Israel would have trouble until the second coming of Messiah. Gabriel followed that discomforting prospect with another reminder of God's sovereignty: "desolations are determined." The reason for war even to the end of the 490 years is as follows: God had already determined irrevocably the extent of desolations necessary to bring Israel back to Himself through its Messiah, Jesus.

The eighth significant thing to note about the Daniel 9 prophecy is this: the seventieth seven of years did not follow immediately after the first sixty-nine sevens of years. There has been a gap of time between the end of the first 483 years (32 A.D.) and the beginning of the last seven years of the 490 prophesied years. Gabriel already referred to two significant events that took place during that gap of time — the death of Messiah in 32 A.D. and the destruction of Jerusalem and the Temple in 70 A.D. (as noted earlier, both of these events transpired after the end of the first 483 years).

There are several evidences for this gap of time. First, if the last seven of the 490 years had followed immediately after the end of the first 483 years (32 A.D.), then the six things that were to happen to Israel and Jerusalem at the end of the 490 years (v. 24) should have happened in 39 A.D. (32 A.D. plus the last seven years). It is a fact that those things have not happened even yet.

Second, verse twenty-seven teaches that abomination will

come with desolation *during* the last seven of the 490 years, but Jesus indicated that this abomination spoken of by Daniel would come shortly before His second coming (Mt. 24:15-21, 29-31). This would mean, then, that the last seven years (the seventieth seven) must also come shortly before Jesus' second coming. Thus, the first 483 years related to Messiah's first coming, but the last seven years relate to His second coming.

Third, the death of Messiah in 32 A.D. and the destruction of Jerusalem and the Temple in 70 A.D. fit within the scope of the 490 year prophecy. Thus, both events were to transpire before the end of the 490 years. In light of this, if the last seven of the 490 years had followed immediately after the end of the first 483 years (32 A.D.), then the 490 years would have ended in 39 A.D., and Jerusalem and the Temple would have been destroyed by 39 A.D. It is a fact, however, that Jerusalem and the Temple were not destroyed until 70 A.D. Only if there were a gap of time between the end of the first sixty-nine sevens of years and the beginning of the seventieth seven of years could this destruction have taken place so late and still be within the scope of the 490 year prophecy.

Fourth, it is not unusual for biblical prophecies to contain gaps of time. For example, Isaiah 9:6 says: "For a child will be born to us" (referring to Messiah's first coming), and "the government will rest on His shoulders" (related to Messiah's second coming). Zechariah 9:9-10 states: "Behold, your king is coming to you; . . . humble, and mounted on a donkey, even on a colt, the foal of a donkey" (referring to Messiah's triumphal entry during His first coming), and "His dominion will be from sea to sea, and from the River to the ends of the earth" (related to Messiah's second coming).

It can be concluded, then, that the gap of time involved with the 490 year prophecy of Daniel 9 started after April 6, 32 A.D., and it will continue until the beginning of the last seven years (the seventieth seven) before the second coming of Jesus Christ. This gap of time has contained many momentous events — not only the crucifixion of Messiah and the destruction of Jerusalem and the Temple, but also the beginning and continuation of the Church and the temporary removal of Israel from the place of covenant blessing that it enjoyed with God throughout its Old Testament history (Rom. 11). This temporary removal happened to Israel because it did not receive its Messiah during His first coming. Israel will be restored to the place of covenant blessing when it receives Jesus as its Messiah and Savior at His second coming at the end of the 490 years. The last seven of the 490 years will play a significant role in bringing Israel to the point where it will be willing to receive Jesus as its Messiah by the time He appears in His second coming.

The ninth significant thing to note concerning the Daniel 9 prophecy is this: the activities of the coming prince or Antichrist during the last seven (seventieth seven) of the 490 years (v. 27). Gabriel dealt with the first sixty-nine sevens of years (483 years) through verse twenty-six. But in verse twenty-seven he dealt with significant events that would transpire during the seventieth seven of years (the last seven years prior to Christ's second coming — the seven years to which many theologians have assigned the designation *The Tribulation Period*).

Some scholars have stated that the *he* of verse twenty-seven referred back to Messiah the Prince, and that verse twenty-seven related things that Messiah would do during His first coming. At least three things militate against that view. First, according to verse twenty-seven, *he* would make a covenant with many people for seven years (*one week* or *one seven*). Nowhere do the Scriptures indicate that Jesus made a covenant with people for seven years. Second, as noted earlier, the context immediately preceding verse twenty-seven related things concerning the coming Roman prince or Antichrist rather than the Messiah. In other words, the Antichrist was the closer antecedent of the *he* in verse twenty-seven. Thus, it is much more natural to regard the *he* as referring back to the Antichrist. Third, other passages that clearly refer to the Antichrist relate activities of his that are parallel to the activities of the *he* of verse twenty-seven.[44] It can be concluded, then, that the *he* of verse twenty-seven referred to the Antichrist.

Gabriel indicated that the Antichrist would do several significant things during the seventieth seven of years. First, he would "make a firm covenant with the many for one seven." Several conclusions can be drawn from this statement. In order to have the authority to make such a covenant, the Antichrist must already possess the position of head king of the confederated Revived Roman Empire before making the covenant (Dan. 7:8, 20, 23-25). In addition, it appears that the establishment of this covenant will be the historic event which will officially begin the seventieth seven of years (The Tribulation Period). Next, since the 490 year prophecy concerns the people of Israel and Jerusalem, "the many" with whom the Antichrist will make this covenant must be the people of Israel who will be living at that time. The language may imply that some of the Jews will be opposed to the covenant, but the majority of Jews will accept it. Another conclusion is that the covenant will be designated to last for seven years. Finally, the language used by Gabriel was quite strong. It indicated that the Antichrist will force or impose a strong covenant upon the many.[45] Apparently this ruler of the Revived Roman Empire in the West will want to have influence or a foothold in the Middle East. In order to accomplish that, he will impose a covenant upon the nation of Israel. That covenant will strongly commit Israel's loyalty to the Antichrist and his empire. It will bind that nation to him so firmly that Israel will practically be an extension of the Antichrist in the Middle East. As a result, Antichrist will regard any attack upon Israel as an attack upon himself; therefore, in this covenant Antichrist will commit himself and his western Roman army to the military protection of Israel. The fact that this future Roman ruler will be able to enforce such a covenant upon Israel is a clear indicator that Israel will still be subject to the whims of Gentile world dominion until the second coming of Christ.

This covenant will make Antichrist appear to be the friend of Israel, but his second activity presented in verse twenty-seven will prove him otherwise. Gabriel said: "but in the middle of the seven he will put a stop to sacrifice and grain offering." This statement implied that, not only will Israel be present as a nation in its homeland, but also it will have a rebuilt Temple in Jerusalem and a reinstatement of its sacrificial system during the last seven years before Christ's second coming. Other passages also indicate a rebuilt Temple for that time (Mt. 24:15, 21, 29-31; 2 Th. 2:2-4). Israel was restored to its homeland and as a nation in 1948, but as yet it has not rebuilt the Temple nor reinstated its Old Testament sacrificial system. But the Scriptures make it clear that it will do so eventually. After the first three and one-half years of the seventieth seven of years have transpired, Antichrist will put a stop to the entire Jewish sacrificial system. The fact that he will be able to do so is an indicator of the great authority that he will have in Israel by the middle of the seventieth seven — the authority to do as he pleases. His stopping of the sacrifices will be the first step in his turning against the Jews to become the greatest human enemy ever to confront Israel.

What will motivate Antichrist to stop the Jewish sacrifices in their Temple? The answer is this: the desire to be worshiped as God. By the middle of the last seven years prior to Christ's return, Antichrist will turn against every form of established worship in order to clear the way for the worship of himself (Dan. 11:36-37; 2 Th. 2:4).

The third activity of Antichrist mentioned in verse twenty-seven will play a significant role in the establishment of the worship of this Roman ruler. Gabriel said: "and on the wing of abominations one who makes desolate." The word translated "wing" refers to the pinnacle or extreme point of something.[46] In light of this, "the wing of abominations" would be the pinnacle or extreme point of abominations. Gabriel was saying that, after Antichrist stops the sacrifices in the Temple, he will commit the pinnacle of all abominations ever performed against the Temples of God in Jerusalem. The Babylonians committed an abomination against the Temple built by Solomon when they destroyed it in 586 B.C. Antiochus Epiphanes performed an abomination against the Temple that was rebuilt after the Babylonian captivity, for he rededicated it to Zeus, had a pagan altar built over the altar of God and instituted the sacrifice of pigs in it between 171 and 165 B.C. The Romans perpetrated an abomination against Herod's Temple when they destroyed it in 70 A.D. But the abomination that Antichrist will commit against the future Temple will be the worst of all these abominations.

The word translated "abominations" means *things detestable*.[47] What action of Antichrist will be so extremely detestable to God? After Antichrist stops the sacrifices of the future Temple, he will magnify himself to the level of deity, take his seat in the Temple, announce that he is God, demand worship of himself by his subjects and set up some detestable thing (probably an image of himself) in the Temple (Dan. 7:8, 11, 20, 25; 11:36-37; 2 Th. 2:3-4; Rev. 13:4-8, 11-17; 19:20; 20:4). Jesus seemed to refer the term "abomination of desolation" in Daniel 9 to the detestable thing that Antichrist will set up in the Temple (Mt. 24:15). From God's viewpoint, that image of the Antichrist, standing where only God is supposed to dwell, will be the pinnacle of all human abominations against His Temple, for it will represent the extreme point of man's humanistic rebellion against the sovereign God — the claim of deity by an ultimate man.

Gabriel warned that, when Antichrist sets up his image in the Temple, he will make something desolate. Since the 490 year prophecy concerns Israel and Jerusalem, they must be the targets of that desolation. Indeed, Jesus warned that, when the Jews will see Antichrist's image standing in the Temple, they should flee out of Judea. He made it clear that rapidity of flight will be so urgent that the Jews should not take time to obtain provisions for their flight. Any hindrances to departure will make things desperate. Jesus told why it will be so urgent for the Jews to flee at that time: "for then there will be a great tribulation, such as has not occurred since the beginning of the world until now, nor ever shall" (Mt. 24:15-21). God revealed to the Apostle John that Israel (represented by a beautiful woman) will have to flee to the wilderness for 1,260 days or three and one-half times in the future (Rev. 12:5-6, 13-15), and that Antichrist, once he makes his arrogant claim of deity, will have authority to act for forty-two months (Rev. 13:5) (compare Daniel 7:25). Since Antichrist will make his claim to be God in the middle of the seventieth seven of years, these 1,260 days, three and one-half times and forty-two months all refer to the latter three and one-half years of the seventieth seven. Tragically, these related passages issue a chilling message — Israel's worst days are still ahead. The latter half of the seventieth seven of years will contain more desolation for Daniel's people than did the Holocaust of World War II. For that reason, the last three and one-half years prior to Christ's second coming have been called "the time of Jacob's trouble" (Jer. 30:4-7). Antichrist will turn upon Israel and will desolate it and Jerusalem.

Gabriel ended the prophecy of Daniel 9 by asserting that Antichrist's desolating of Israel will have a limit. It would continue "until a complete destruction, one that is decreed, is poured out." Antichrist will cause horror until all the judgment that God has sovereignly determined has been administered. Upon whom will this divine judgment be poured out? Gabriel's answer can be translated two different ways: either *on the one who makes desolate* (referring to Antichrist) or *on the desolate* (referring to Israel and Jerusalem).[48] If Gabriel had the former concept in mind, then he was saying the following: Antichrist will be able to desolate Israel and Jerusalem until the complete judgment that God has sovereignly determined for him has been poured out upon him. As noted earlier, Antichrist will indeed suffer severe divine judgment (Dan. 7:25-26; 11:45; 2 Th. 2:8; Rev. 19:19-20). If Gabriel had the latter concept in mind, then he was stating this: Antichrist will be able to desolate Israel and Jerusalem until the complete chastening which God has sovereignly determined for them has been poured out upon them. As noted earlier, God has already determined the extent of desolations necessary to bring Israel back to Himself through its Messiah, Jesus. Antichrist's persecution of Israel will complete those decreed desolations. Israel's worst time of suffering at the hands of Antichrist will be God's sovereign means of breaking that nation's stubborn rebellion, shattering its unbelief and bringing it to faith in Jesus Christ, so that the six blessings of verse twenty-four can take place. God's judgment of Antichrist and chastening of Israel will be completed at the same time — at the end of the 490 years when Christ returns in His second coming. Thus, Antichrist will be able to desolate Israel and Jerusalem until then.

# CONCLUDING REMARKS

This new revelation delivered by Gabriel offered Daniel the twofold prospect of despair and hope. Jerusalem would be rebuilt with its defenses after the Babylonian captivity, but that would not be the end of Israel's troubles. In spite of the fact that this prophecy informed Israel of the exact time when Messiah would be present to present Himself as Prince to the nation, the Jews would have Him put to death. As a result of their rejection of the Messiah in His first coming, Israel would miss the opportunity of lasting peace at that time and would bring upon itself many more desolations — including the destruction of Jerusalem and the Temple by the Romans in 70 A.D. and the final but worst desolations by Antichrist, the last Roman ruler. Once all the chastening which God had decreed for Israel and Jerusalem would run its course, then Israel would return to God forever and experience blessing. Ultimately there would be blessing, but Israel would have to experience a long time (including 490 decreed years) of chastening to reach that blessing.

In light of the revelation in Daniel 9, it can be concluded that Israel's present independence and possession of Jerusalem is only a temporary lull in what is to be the norm for that nation and city until the end of the 490 years. In essence, it is a calm before the worst storm that Israel will ever experience. Jesus said that Jerusalem will be trampled under foot by the Gentiles until the times of the Gentiles will be fulfilled (Lk. 21:24). Daniel 2 and 7 indicated that those times will not be fulfilled until the second coming of Christ.

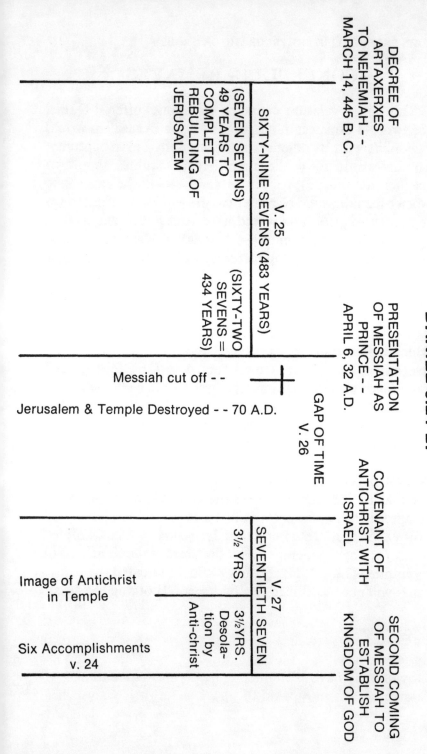

# THE PROPHECY OF SEVENTY SEVENS (490 YEARS)
## DANIEL 9:24-27

DECREE OF ARTAXERXES TO NEHEMIAH - - MARCH 14, 445 B.C.

SIXTY-NINE SEVENS (483 YEARS)
V. 25

(SEVEN SEVENS) 49 YEARS TO COMPLETE REBUILDING OF JERUSALEM

(SIXTY-TWO SEVENS = 434 YEARS)

PRESENTATION OF MESSIAH AS PRINCE - - APRIL 6, 32 A.D.

Messiah cut off - -

Jerusalem & Temple Destroyed - - 70 A.D.

GAP OF TIME V. 26

COVENANT OF ANTICHRIST WITH ISRAEL

SECOND COMING OF MESSIAH TO ESTABLISH KINGDOM OF GOD

V. 27 SEVENTIETH SEVEN

3½ YRS.

3½ YRS. Desolation by Anti-christ

Image of Antichrist in Temple

Six Accomplishments v. 24

**10**

# THE INTRODUCTION
# TO THE LAST REVELATION
## Chapters 10:1-11:1

## A NOTE OF EXPLANATION

Chapters ten through twelve contain the last revelation
received and recorded by Daniel. That revelation presented
God's rule over Israel in the near and far future. The first
segment of these three chapters (10:1-11:1) contains the
introduction to the new revelation. This introduction
explains how Daniel received the revelation and presents
some fascinating incidents related to the delivering of the
new truth to Daniel.

## DANIEL'S CONDITION (10:1-3)

*In the third year of Cyrus king of Persia a message was revealed
to Daniel, who was named Belteshazzar; and the message was
true and one of great conflict, but he understood the message
and had an understanding of the vision. In those days I, Daniel,
had been mourning for three entire weeks. I did not eat any tasty
food, nor did meat or wine enter my mouth, nor did I use any
ointment at all, until the entire three weeks were completed.*

Daniel received the last revelation in 536 B.C.[1] This was
approximately two years after King Cyrus officially ended
the Babylonian captivity of the Jews.[2] Daniel did not return
home to Palestine with his fellow Jews. His remaining in
Babylon may have been due in part to his advanced age —
by then he was in his mid to upper eighties. However, his

important position in the government probably was the main reason for his continuation in Babylon. He could use his influence for the good of Israel as long as he remained there.[3]

Because the new revelation contained things which would be hard to believe, Daniel emphasized that it was true — it was to be believed. The revelation dealt with "great conflict." It presented great warfare that would take place beyond Daniel's day — warfare between nations, but also great angelic warfare behind the scenes of international events. This conflict would threaten the existence of Israel. Daniel declared that he understood this new revelation. Apparently it helped him understand the vision of chapter eight also (much of the new revelation was related to things portrayed in that earlier vision).

Before Daniel received the new revelation he had been mourning by fasting for twenty-one days. For three entire weeks he did not consume delicacies or regular foods and abstained from anointing himself (anointing was associated with joy — Prov. 27:9).[4] Daniel fasted because he was so intent on understanding and on humbling himself before God (v. 12). Apparently he still couldn't understand the continued suffering of Israel portrayed in the vision of chapter eight; therefore, he was humbling himself with a mournful attitude on behalf of Israel.

## DANIEL'S VISION OF A
## HEAVENLY BEING (10:4-9)

*And on the twenty-fourth day of the first month, while I was by the bank of the great river, that is, the Tigris, I lifted my eyes and looked, and behold, there was a certain man dressed in linen, whose waist was girded with a belt of pure gold of Uphaz. His body also was like beryl, his face had the appearance of lightning, his eyes were like flaming torches, his arms and feet like the gleam of polished bronze, and the sound of his words*

> like the sound of a tumult. Now I, Daniel, alone saw the vision, while the men who were with me did not see the vision; nevertheless, a great dread fell on them, and they ran away to hide themselves. So I was left alone and saw this great vision; yet no strength was left in me, for my natural color turned to a deathly pallor, and I retained no strength. But I heard the sound of his words; and as soon as I heard the sound of his words, I fell into a deep sleep on my face, with my face to the ground.

One day in April, while Daniel stood beside the Tigris River (there probably on government business), a vision of a unique being standing above the river suddenly appeared to him.[5] Although this being was in the form of a man, he certainly was not a mere human being. His appearance clearly marked him as a supernatural, heavenly being. His body was clothed with linen (symbol of holiness — Lev. 16:4), and a girdle of pure gold was around his waist. The parts of his body that could be seen had the appearance of a beautiful gem that gleamed like polished bronze. His face had the brilliance of lightning, and his eyes resembled burning torches. His voice sounded like the roaring of a great crowd or rushing waters.[6] The appearance of this being was awesome, emphasizing holiness, purity, beauty, power, penetrating perception and authority.

A crucial question must be asked at this point — who was this heavenly being? Since he obviously was not a human being, he had to be either a divine being or an angelic being. The description of this being corresponds exactly with the description of the glorified Christ as seen by the Apostle John (Rev. 1:13-17; 2:18). It would appear, then, that Daniel saw the eternal Christ in a preincarnate appearance.[7]

This view identifying the heavenly being with Christ does have some problems. First, an evil angel (the prince of the kingdom of Persia — v. 13) hindered the progress of the heavenly being for twenty-one days. Certainly no angel would have the power to do that to the Son of God. This problem could be answered as follows: it is true that no

angel would have such power; however, Christ could
sovereignly permit an angel to do this, if He had a purpose
for doing so. Certainly Christ sovereignly permitted mere
human beings to crucify Him, because it suited His purpose
(Mt. 26:53-54). In addition, this problem is no greater than
the one of Satan waging war against God throughout most
of world history. God could have crushed Satan's opposition immediately but had a sovereign purpose for not doing
so.

A second problem is this: even if Christ were to permit
Himself to be hindered, would not an evil angel be too
frightened of His power to approach Him with a negative
purpose? This problem could be answered in this manner:
Satan, who is an evil angel, was not too frightened to
approach Christ with the negative purpose of tempting
Him.

A third problem is the fact that Michael, a good angel,
came to help this heavenly being when the prince of Persia
withstood him. Certainly Christ would not need the help of
a good angel in any circumstance. The reply to this problem
is as follows: it is true that Christ does not need the help of
good angels; however, He could choose to allow such help, if
that help would suit His sovereign purpose. Christ accepted
the help of angels after His temptation by Satan (Mt. 4:11)
and in conjunction with His agony in Gethsemane (Lk.
22:43). In addition, angels will assist the glorified Christ in
His work at the second coming (Mt. 13:40-43, 49-50; 24:30-
31).

Although there are problems with the view that says the
heavenly being was Christ, those problems are not in-
superable. In light of the exact correspondence of the
description of this heavenly being with that of the glorified
Christ in Revelation, it seems best to conclude that Daniel
saw the Son of God.

Daniel's companions did not see the vision of Christ, but

they sensed that something unusual was transpiring. The supernatural presence of Christ caused such a strong sensation of dread to come upon them that they ran to hide. This was similar to what Paul's companions experienced when the glorified Christ appeared to him on the road to Damascus (Acts 9:7).

Daniel alone saw the vision of Christ, and it overwhelmed him. In spite of the fact that Daniel was a spiritual giant among men, this sudden confrontation with a vision of deity caused him to lose his strength. His usual stately appearance became distorted with "a grotesque wrenching of facial features."[8] The word translated "deathly pallor" is the word that was used for the disfigurement of Messiah's face in Isaiah 52:14.[9] As soon as Daniel heard the roar of Christ's voice, he fainted face downward to the ground. The Apostle John reacted the same way when he saw the glorified Christ (Rev. 1:17). These experiences of God's saints when confronted by deity should strike terror in the heart of rebellious man and cause him to adopt an attitude of awe, reverence and worship for God.

## THE FIRST STRENGTHENING OF DANIEL AND STATEMENT OF PURPOSE BY THE HEAVENLY BEING (10:10-17)

*Then behold, a hand touched me and set me trembling on my hands and knees. And he said to me, "O Daniel, man of high esteem, understand the words that I am about to tell you and stand upright, for I have now been sent to you." And when he had spoken this word to me, I stood up trembling. Then he said to me, "Do not be afraid, Daniel, for from the first day that you set your heart on understanding this and on humbling yourself before your God, your words were heard, and I have come in response to your words. But the prince of the kingdom of Persia was withstanding me for twenty-one days; then behold, Michael, one of the chief princes, came to help me, for I had been left there with the kings of Persia. Now I have come to give you an understanding of what will happen to your people in the latter days, for the vision pertains to the days yet future." And when he had spoken to me according to these words, I turned my face toward the ground and became speechless. And behold, one who resembled a human being was touching my lips; then I opened my mouth and spoke, and said to him who was standing before me, "O my lord, as a result of the vision anguish has come upon me, and I have retained no strength. For how can such a servant of my lord talk with such as my lord? As for me, there remains just now no strength in me, nor has any breath been left in me."*

By touching Daniel Christ revived him to the point of getting him to his knees. But Daniel was so unsteady that he swayed to and fro on his hands and knees.[10] In order to encourage Daniel, Christ told him that he was greatly beloved by God. Daniel was exhorted to pay attention to Christ's words and to stand upright, because the heavenly being had been sent to Daniel by God. The implication of the exhortation was this: since God had shown so much favor to Daniel, he should be willing to exert himself to stand up and listen. Daniel did rise to his feet, but he was still unsteady.

Noting that Daniel continued to tremble with fear, Christ reassured him by telling him not to be afraid. The reason for not fearing was the following special favor that God had already exercised toward Daniel: on the very first day of Daniel's mourning, God had heard his prayer and had responded to it by sending Christ to him. Daniel had been asking for understanding of the vision in chapter eight.

Although Christ had been sent on the first day of Daniel's mourning, He did not reach Daniel until after the period of mourning had ended. The reason for Christ's delay was this: a high ranking evil angel, whom Satan had assigned to influence Medo-Persia against Israel, had detained Him for twenty-one days. Since Daniel was a Jew and could benefit Israel through his high position in the Medo-Persian government, this angel did not want Christ to deliver the new revelation about Israel's future to him. Because this opposition by this angelic prince left Christ occupied with the policies of the Medo-Persian kings (Cyrus and his subkings), Michael, one of God's chief angelic princes, came to take up the battle against this evil angel. Michael holds the high rank of archangel (Jude 9). Just as Satan had assigned a high ranking evil angel to be the prince of Medo-Persia, so God has assigned Michael to be the prince of Israel (Dan. 10:21). Michael has the task of fighting Satan and his evil angels when the welfare of the Israelites is at stake (Jude 9; Rev. 12:1-9). Michael's coming to fight the prince of Persia freed Christ to come to Daniel.

Christ told Daniel that His purpose for coming was to reveal to him what would happen to Israel in "the latter days." Christ explained that expression by indicating that the revelation pertained to the days yet future — the days beyond Daniel's day. Jacob used the same expression to refer to the days that were yet future beyond his time (Gen. 49:1), and it was used in Daniel 2:28 to refer to the days that were future beyond Nebuchadnezzar's time. As used here in Daniel 10, "the latter days" basically would be parallel to the expression "the latter portion of the indignation" which covered the span of history from the 530's B.C. to the second coming of Christ (Dan. 8:19). Thus, the revelation contained in Daniel 11 and 12 would fit into that time span.

It should be noted that Christ said the revelation would show what would happen to Israel in the future. Thus, its major concern would be the destiny of that nation.

While Christ was speaking, Daniel began to experience weakness again. He dropped his face downward and found it impossible to speak. Christ touched his lips to enable him to speak. As Daniel spoke, he called Christ "my lord," thereby vocalizing his recognition of Christ's superiority. He explained that the reason for his weakness and inability to speak was the intense pain caused by Christ's supernatural appearance.

## THE SECOND STRENGTHENING OF DANIEL AND STATEMENT OF PURPOSE BY THE HEAVENLY BEING (10:18-11:1)

*Then this one with human appearance touched me again and strengthened me. And he said, "O man of high esteem, do not be afraid. Peace be with you; take courage and be courageous!" Now as soon as he spoke to me, I received strength and said, "May my lord speak, for you have strengthened me." Then he said, "Do you understand why I came to you? But I shall now return to fight against the prince of Persia; so I am going forth, and behold, the prince of Greece is about to come. However, I will tell you what is inscribed in the writing of truth. (Yet there is no one who stands firmly with me against these forces except Michael your prince. And in the first year of Darius the Mede I arose to be an encouragement and protection for him.)*

Christ touched Daniel again and imparted more strength to him. He continued to make statements of encouragement and commanded him to be strong. The more Christ spoke these words of encouragement, the stronger Daniel became by degrees. Finally Daniel was strong enough to exhort the Lord to continue His speech which had been interrupted when Daniel's face dropped toward the ground.

Christ asked Daniel if he understood why He had come to him. This was His way of emphasizing His earlier statement of purpose (v. 14) and of making sure that Daniel had caught that purpose while in his weakened condition.

The Lord told Daniel that, after He would finish revealing to him what God had prewritten concerning the future, He would return to fight against Satan's prince of Persia again. As soon as He would be finished with that prince, He would have to fight with the prince of Greece. The implication was that, when Medo-Persia would fall to Greece, the prince of Persia would be replaced by another evil angelic prince —

the prince of Greece, whom Satan would assign to that new kingdom of Gentile world dominion to influence its policies against Israel.

Christ indicated that He and Michael, God's angelic prince of Israel, were the only two supernatural beings who opposed such evil angelic forces as the prince of Persia and the prince of Greece on behalf of Israel. As an example of their teamwork, Christ related how He had acted to strengthen and protect Michael during the first year of Darius the Mede (538 B.C.). That was a crucial year. It was the year immediately following Medo-Persia's conquest of Babylon. That conquest made the Jews subject to Medo-Persian control. Thus, in 538 B.C. King Cyrus and his subkings would have been deciding their policy toward Israel. Apparently Satan's prince of Persia saw this as an opportune time to turn the kings of Medo-Persia against Israel from the very outset. In order to prevent Michael's interfering with his plans, he must have attacked him with everything in his arsenal. This fierce attack necessitated Christ coming to the aid of the prince of Israel. That Christ and Michael succeeded in defeating these early efforts of the prince of Persia is seen in the fact that King Cyrus adopted a favorable policy toward Israel. 538 B.C. was the year in which Cyrus ended the Babylonian captivity of the Jews and permitted them to return home to start rebuilding.[11]

## CONCLUDING REMARKS

Daniel 10 gives a brief glimpse into an area of reality concerning which most human beings are totally unaware — the role of Christ and angels in international affairs. Both God and Satan have assigned powerful angels to influence rulers and nations in their policies — particularly in their policies for or against Israel. Behind the scenes of international events there rages great supernatural conflict invisible to the human eye.

Christ's statement to the effect that the revelation He would deliver to Daniel was "inscribed in the writing of truth" (v. 21) carries with it the idea that God has prewritten the course of history. This again emphasized the sovereignty of God.

# 11

## GOD'S RULE OVER ISRAEL IN THE NEAR AND FAR FUTURE DEMONSTRATED
### Chapters 11:2-12:3

### A NOTE OF INTEREST

The first major section (11:2-35) of the new revelation given by Christ to Daniel has been one of the most controversial portions of Scripture. After tracing in survey fashion four Persian rulers and Alexander the Great of Greece (vv. 2-4), the passage gave specific details concerning the Ptolemies of Egypt and the Seleucids of Syria — the rulers of the two major divisions of Alexander's Grecian kingdom (vv. 5-35). Because of the mass of specific details that have been fulfilled so accurately, destructive critics have argued that this portion of Daniel could not have been written in Daniel's day, many years before the events described. They insist that this passage was written after the events, because no one could possibly foretell so much specific detail so accurately so far in advance. In other words, they contend that this was a record of history, not predictive prophecy.[1] The claim that no one could foretell so much detail so accurately so far in advance is a denial of the sovereignty of God. As noted earlier, Christ declared that God has prewritten the course of history (10:21). While it is true that no human being would have the ability to foretell so much detail so accurately, the God who is sovereign over history would have precisely that ability. Thus, the critics'

denial of the prophetic nature of this passage is simply
another expression of man's rejection of God's sovereign
rule.

The text of this commentary will explain how Christ's
prophecies to Daniel contained in verses two through thirty-
five were fulfilled historically.

## THE PROPHETIC PREFACE
## OF THE NEW REVELATION (11:2-4)

*"And now I will tell you the truth. Behold, three more kings are
going to arise in Persia. Then a fourth will gain far more riches
than all of them; as soon as he becomes strong through his
riches, he will arouse the whole empire against the realm of
Greece. And a mighty king will arise, and he will rule with great
authority and do as he pleases. But as soon as he has arisen, his
kingdom will be broken up and parcelled out toward the four
points of the compass, though not to his own descendants, nor
according to his authority which he wielded; for his sovereignty
will be uprooted and given to others besides them.*

When Christ gave the new revelation to Daniel (536
B.C.), Cyrus was the head king of Medo-Persia. Christ
declared that after Cyrus there would be three more Medo-
Persian kings before the fourth successor. The three kings
were Cambyses (529-522 B.C.), Pseudo-Smerdis (522-521
B.C.) and Darius I Hystaspes (521-486 B.C.).[2] The fourth
successor of Cyrus was Xerxes I (486-465 B.C.).[3] Xerxes
amassed great wealth and prepared a huge army over a four
year period in order to invade Greece in 480 B.C.[4] The
expedition against Greece ended in disaster for Persia.

Although there were several more Medo-Persian kings
after Xerxes, Christ traced the history of that kingdom's
rulers only to the king who launched the massive attack
against Greece. The reason He did so was as follows: that
attack of Greece by Xerxes was one of the major factors
motivating Alexander the Great and the Greeks to attack

Medo-Persia almost 150 years later, thus, Christ uses Xerxes' invasion of Greece as the foundation for introducing Alexander.[5]

The "mighty king" (vv. 3-4) was Alexander the Great, the Macedonian who led the Greek-Macedonian army in conquest of Medo-Persia and many other lands beginning in 334 B.C. Alexander was a military and administrative genius. He was able to rule and conquer a vast territory covering some 11,000 miles. However, no sooner did he become the sole ruler of the known ancient world than he was cut down by death at age thirty-two (323 B.C.). Neither of his sons succeeded him, for both were murdered.[6] Through time four Greek generals divided Alexander's kingdom into four parts, but none of them ever ruled with the same authority as Alexander.

## THE WARS BETWEEN THE KINGS OF THE SOUTH AND THE NORTH FOR DOMINION OVER ISRAEL (11:5-20)

*"Then the king of the South will grow strong, along with one of his princes who will gain ascendancy over him and obtain dominion; his domain will be a great dominion indeed. And after some years they will form an alliance, and the daughter of the king of the South will come to the king of the North to carry out a peaceful arrangement. But she will not retain her position of power, nor will he remain with his power, but she will be given up, along with those who brought her in, and the one who sired her, as well as he who supported her in those times. But one of the descendants of her line will arise in his place, and he will come against their army and enter the fortress of the king of the North, and he will deal with them and display great strength. And also their gods with their metal images and their precious vessels of silver and gold he will take into captivity to Egypt, and he on his part will refrain from attacking the king of the North for some years. Then the latter will enter the realm of the king of the South, but will return to his own land. And his sons will mobilize and assemble a multitude of great forces; and one of*

*them will keep on coming and overflow and pass through, that
he may again wage war up to his very fortress. And the king of
the South will be enraged and go forth and fight with the king of
the North. Then the latter will raise a great multitude, but that
multitude will be given into the hand of the former. When the
multitude is carried away, his heart will be lifted up, and he will
cause tens of thousands to fall; yet he will not prevail. For the
king of the North will again raise a greater multitude than the
former, and after an interval of some years he will press on with a
great army and much equipment. Now in those times many will
rise up against the king of the South; the violent ones among
your people will also lift themselves up in order to fulfill the
vision, but they will fall down. Then the king of the North will
come, cast up a siege mound, and capture a well fortified city;
and the forces of the South will not stand their ground, not even
their choicest troops, for there will be no strength to make a
stand. But he who comes against him will do as he pleases, and
no one will be able to withstand him; he will also stay for a time
in the Beautiful Land, with destruction in his hand. And he will
set his face to come with the power of his whole kingdom,
bringing with him a proposal of peace which he will put into
effect; he will also give him the daughter of women to ruin it. But
she will not take a stand for him or be on his side. Then he will
turn his face to the coastlands and capture many. But a
commander will put a stop to his scorn against him; moreover,
he will repay him for his scorn. So he will turn his face toward
the fortresses of his own land, but he will stumble and fall and be
found no more. Then in his place one will arise who will send an
oppressor through the Jewel of his kingdom; yet within a few
days he will be shattered, though neither in anger nor in battle.*

Of the four divisions of Alexander's kingdom, only two
proved to be significant in the ancient world — the division
ruled by the Ptolemies which headquartered in Egypt and
the division ruled by the Seleucids which headquartered in
Syria. Since Egypt was south of Israel, Christ called the
rulers of Egypt "the king of the South." Since Syria was
north of Israel, He called the rulers of Syria "the king of the
North."

The king of the south (v. 5) was Ptolemy I Soter who ruled

Egypt from 323 to 285 B.C.[7] Seleucus I Nicator served him for several years, but in 312 B.C. Seleucus became ruler of Babylonia.[8] Through time Seleucus also gained control of Syria, southern Asia Minor and the Iranian Plateau. This made him the ruler of a much larger kingdom than that of Ptolemy Soter.

Several years after Ptolemy I Soter and Seleucus I Nicator, two new kings, Ptolemy II Philadelphus (285-246 B.C.) of Egypt and Antiochus II Theos (261-246 B.C.) of Syria, formed an alliance. Ptolemy's daughter, Berenice, was married to Antiochus to bind the alliance. Ptolemy forced Antiochus to divorce his first wife, Laodice, in order to marry Berenice. The marriage did not last, however. When Ptolemy died a few years later, Antiochus abandoned Berenice and took back Laodice. Laodice was so jealous over her divorce that she had her husband, Berenice, Berenice's baby and all those who had accompanied Berenice from Egypt murdered.[9]

Berenice's brother, Ptolemy III Euergetes (246-221 B.C.), succeeded his father as king of Egypt. To avenge his sister's murder he marched north, defeated the Syrian army, invaded Syria and put Laodice to death. He conquered large areas of the Seleucid kingdom and carried back to Egypt 40,000 talents of silver and 2,500 idols. He remained more powerful than the Syrians for a number of years. However, around 240 B.C., the new Syrian king, Seleucus Callinicus, made a retaliatory invasion against Egypt. He was defeated and had to return home (vv. 7-9).[10]

The sons of Seleucus Callinicus, Seleucus III Ceraunus (226-223 B.C.) and Antiochus III the Great (223-187 B.C.), gathered a huge Syrian army together.[11] Seleucus was killed in an early battle in Asia Minor, so Antiochus took charge of the army. He made great rapid conquests, retaking Syrian territory held by Egypt. By 219 B.C. he had conquered into parts of Israel and the Transjordan.

Antiochus let up on the campaign in that year but returned to the offensive again in 217 B.C. This time he conquered south to the Egyptian fortress at Raphia.[12] All this time Ptolemy IV Philopator (221-203 B.C.), the king of Egypt, sat idly by involved in a life of luxury and ease (v. 10).[13]

Finally Ptolemy got angry with the advances toward Egypt by Antiochus. He assembled an army consisting of 70,000 infantry, 5,000 cavalry and 73 elephants and marched against Antiochus.[14] Antiochus had 72,000 infantry, 6,000 cavalry and 102 elephants.[15] In 217 B.C. the two armies clashed at Raphia.[16] Egypt won a great victory. Antiochus lost 10,000 infantry, 300 cavalry and five elephants through death and 4,000 prisoners through capture.[17] Ptolemy became very proud over his victory, but he did not press his advantage. Instead of retaking all lost territory from Syria, he returned home to his life of ease (vv. 11-12).[18]

In 203 B.C. Ptolemy Philopator and his wife died. Their son, Ptolemy V Epiphanes (203-181 B.C.), became king of Egypt when only four years old. Antiochus the Great saw this as the opportune time to retaliate against Egypt. He marched south with a larger, well-equipped army which he had developed through some successful eastern campaigns during the fourteen years since Raphia (v. 13).[19]

Antiochus did not fight Egypt alone. He made a league with Philip V of Macedonia, Egyptian rebels who opposed their child-king and Jewish men of violence who resented Egypt's influence in Israel. Egypt controlled Israel again after the battle at Raphia in 217 B.C. The Jewish rebels decided to help Antiochus the Great take Israel away from Egypt.[20] They thought that their alliance with Syria would aid Israel, but instead it brought their nation into Syria's grasp and made it subject to the horrors that Antiochus Epiphanes would bring upon it in later years. Thus, their action helped to bring about the fulfillment of the vision in

Daniel 8 (v. 14).

In 198 B.C. Antiochus the Great conquered a leading Egyptian general, Scopas, by besieging and conquering Sidon, the fortress city in which Scopas was located. Three attempts to rescue the besieged Scopas by three chosen Egyptian generals (Eropas, Menacles, Damoyenus) failed. This victory for Syria ended Egypt's rule in Israel (v. 15).[21]

Antiochus now had no opposition for some time. He had a free hand to do what he wanted in the Middle East. He came to Israel and took complete control of that land (the word translated "destruction" means *completeness* and referred to Israel being completely in his hand).[22] Antiochus treated the Jews well — he released Jerusalem from taxes for three years and sent money to the Temple (v. 16).[23]

By this time the rising power of Rome was beginning to threaten Syria's expansionist program. In light of this, Antiochus decided that he dare not risk a costly military invasion against the land of Egypt itself. Instead, he determined to bring Egypt under his control through a treaty. The threatening power of his enlarged kingdom gave him leverage to make Egypt agreeable to such a treaty. As part of this treaty, Antiochus married his daughter, Cleopatra, to the Egyptian king, Ptolemy Epiphanes, in 197 B.C. Ptolemy was about ten years old at that time.[24] Antiochus planned for his daughter to work for him against her husband. She was supposed to work from the inside to ruin Egypt as an opponent of Syria. The scheme didn't work. Cleopatra constantly sided with her husband against her father (v. 17).[25]

Beginning in 197 B.C., Antiochus the Great conquered several Aegean Sea islands and portions of Asia Minor and Thrace. He even invaded and conquered parts of Greece. Rome was seeking to control these areas, so Antiochus boasted concerning what he was doing to Roman interests. Rome sent the Roman general, Lucius Cornelius Scipio

(Scipio Asiaticus), to deal with him. In 191 B.C. Scipio forced him out of Greece. In 190 B.C. Scipio defeated Antiochus terribly in the Battle of Magnesia in Asia Minor. In 188 B.C. the Romans forced him to relinquish all of Asia Minor.[26] Now the Romans boasted concerning what they were doing to Antiochus' interests (v. 18).

Antiochus the Great had been defeated so soundly that he had to withdraw to the protection of his own land, Syria, never again to conquer the strongholds of other lands. In 187 B.C. he was killed while trying to rob a temple in Elam in order to replenish his exhausted treasury (v. 19).[27]

Antiochus the Great was succeeded by his son, Seleucus IV Philopator (187-176 B.C.). The Romans required him to pay a 1,000 talent tribute each year. This forced him to levy heavy taxes on the peoples of his kingdom. Seleucus sent his prime minister, Heliodorus, to Jerusalem to take the wealth of the Temple treasury. A short time after this, Seleucus suddenly and mysteriously died, possibly of poisoning in 176 B.C. (v. 20).[28]

## PROPHECIES CONCERNING ANTIOCHUS EPIPHANES (11:21-35)

*"And in his place a despicable person will arise, on whom the honor of kingship has not been conferred, but he will come in a time of tranquility and seize the kingdom by intrigue. And the overflowing forces will be flooded away before him and shattered, and also the prince of the covenant. And after an alliance is made with him he will practice deception, and he will go up and gain power with a small force of people. In a time of tranquility he will enter the richest parts of the realm, and he will accomplish what his fathers never did, nor his ancestors; he will distribute plunder, booty, and possessions among them, and he will devise his schemes against strongholds, but only for a time. And he will stir up his strength and courage against the king of the South with a large army; so the king of the South will mobilize an extremely large and mighty army for war; but he will*

*not stand, for schemes will be devised against him. And those who eat his choice food will destroy him, and his army will overflow, but many will fall down slain. As for both kings, their hearts will be intent on evil, and they will speak lies to each other at the same table; but it will not succeed, for the end is still to come at the appointed time. Then he will return to his land with much plunder; but his heart will be set against the holy covenant, and he will take action and then return to his own land. At the appointed time he will return and come into the South, but this last time it will not turn out the way it did before. For ships of Kittim will come against him; therefore he will be disheartened, and will return and become enraged at the holy covenant and take action; so he will come back and show regard for those who forsake the holy covenant. And forces from him will arise, desecrate the sanctuary fortress, and do away with the regular sacrifice. And they will set up the abomination of desolation. And by smooth words he will turn to godlessness those who act wickedly toward the covenant, but the people who know their God will display strength and take action. And those who have insight among the people will give understanding to the many; yet they will fall by sword and by flame, by captivity and by plunder, for many days. Now when they fall they will be granted a little help, and many will join with them in hypocrisy. And some of those who have insight will fall, in order to refine, purge, and make them pure, until the end time; because it is still to come at the appointed time.*

Seleucus IV Philopator was succeeded by Antiochus IV Epiphanes (175-164 B.C.) as king of Syria.[29] Antiochus was so contemptible that his comtemporaries nicknamed him "Epimanes" (*madman*) instead of the title that he gave himself ("Theos Epiphanes" — *the God Made Manifest*).[30,31] Antiochus was not the rightful heir to the throne. One of Seleucus' two sons was the rightful heir. However, when Antiochus learned about Seleucus' death, he came to Syria and took the throne, not by waging war, but by the use of flattery and intrigue (v. 21).[32]

Early in Antiochus' rule Egypt prepared an army to march against him. When Antiochus learned about this, he marched his Syrian army south to attack the Egyptian army.

Antiochus completely routed this opponent in 170 B.C. at a
battle which took place on the Mediterranean seacoast
halfway between Gaza and the Nile delta.³³ Antiochus
allowed Onias III, the high priest of Israel, to be deposed
and replaced by Onias' brother, Jason. Jason had wanted
Greek culture established in Israel, but Onias had opposed
this (2 Macc. 4:7-15). Onias was called "the prince of the
covenant," because it was the high priest's responsibility to
see that Israel kept its covenant with God (v. 22).³⁴

Antiochus offered friendship to Egypt in order to get it to
let down its guard against him. Having accomplished this,
he then proceeded to try to gain control of Egypt through
deceitful means. In spite of the small size to which Rome had
reduced his Syrian kingdom, Antiochus began to rise in
power (v. 23).³⁵

Antiochus robbed the richest parts of his own kingdom
when they did not expect to be plundered. He did not
squander this wealth upon himself, as his ancestors had
done. Instead, he very generously distributed it among his
poorer subjects in order to gain their support (1 Macc. 3:30).
He planned to take Egypt's fortresses to serve his ends, but
God had decreed only so much time for him (v. 24).³⁶

Antiochus and Ptolemy VI Philometor (181-145 B.C.)
battled each other with huge armies when Antiochus
invaded Egyptian territory. Ptolemy was soundly defeated,
because some of his own men from his royal court plotted
against him and aided the Syrian enemy. Many Egyptian
soldiers were killed. Ptolemy was overthrown as king of
Egypt and taken captive by Antiochus. Some Egyptians
crowned Ptolemy Philometor's brother, Ptolemy VII Euergetes, as king of Egypt in Alexandria. In light of this new
development, Antiochus pretended to befriend captured
Philometor in order to obtain his help against Euergetes.
Antiochus promised to reconquer Egypt for Philometor to
restore him as king. Philometor pretended to believe

Antiochus. But both intended to use the other to gain control of all Egypt. The intentions of both failed. Antiochus did conquer the city of Memphis but failed to take Alexandria. He returned home without taking all of Egypt. Philometor became king of Memphis but had to settle for a joint rule of Egypt with his brother.[37] Their intentions failed because God's appointed time for the end of the Syrian-Egyptian wars had not yet come.[38] God in His sovereignty was using these wars as part of His indignation against Israel. Since Israel was located between these two Gentile powers, it suffered greatly during the course of these wars (vv. 25-27).

Although he had not conquered all of Egypt, Antiochus did take much wealth from it to carry home to Syria. Before this Egyptian campaign, Antiochus had removed Jason as high priest of Israel and replaced him with Menelaus. Menelaus had sought this position by offering Antiochus higher tribute money (2 Macc. 4:23-27). While Antiochus was fighting in Egypt, Jason heard a false rumor to the effect that Antiochus was dead. Jason raised a Jewish force and attacked Jerusalem to overthrow Menelaus. Menelaus beat off the attack, but, as Antiochus returned home through Israel, he determined to teach the rebel Jews a lesson. He slaughtered many Jews, sold many into slavery, plundered the Temple of its valuable contents and carried these sacred things of God to Syria (1 Macc. 1:20-28; 2 Macc. 5:5-21). This showed his personal contempt for Israel's covenant relationship with God (v. 28).

When Antiochus learned that Ptolemy Philometor had formed a coalition with Ptolemy Euergetes to rule Egypt jointly, he felt betrayed. As a result, he invaded Egypt a third time in 168 B.C. Christ told Daniel that the time of this invasion had been appointed sovereignly by God. This third invasion did not have the successful outcome for Antiochus that the first invasion of 170 B.C. had had. While

Antiochus was besieging Alexandria, the Romans sent
Popilius Laenas with many soldiers in trireme ships to
prevent Antiochus from taking Egypt. When Laenas told
Antiochus that the Roman Senate wanted him to leave
Egypt, Antiochus stalled for time. Laenas drew a circle
around Antiochus and told him to decide either to leave
Egypt or to fight Rome before leaving the circle. Antiochus
was so fearful of Rome's power that he left Egypt, but very
reluctantly and dejected. With great bitterness of heart he
decided to vent his wrath upon the people of Israel who were
opposing his efforts to enforce Greek culture upon the
nation. He gave special favors to Menelaus and his apostate
Jewish followers who were rejecting the true worship of God
in favor of the Hellenization process (vv. 29-30) (1 Macc.
1:11-15; 2 Macc. 4:4-17).[39]

Antiochus ordered his general, Apollonius, to occupy
Jerusalem with Syrian troops for the purpose of stamping
out every trace of Judaism and replacing it with Hellenism.
The Syrian soldiers stationed themselves in the Temple and
the fortress which guarded the Temple. An edict was made
that all nationalities in Antiochus' kingdom were to be fused
into one people. All were to worship Greek deities. An
Athenian philosopher was sent to Jerusalem to supervise the
enforcement of the edict. The regular Temple sacrifices to
God were stopped. Syrian soldiers and harlots performed
licentious heathen rites in the Temple courts. Pigs were
sacrificed to Greek gods in the Temple. Jews were required
to take part in a drunken orgy in honor of Bacchus, the god
of wine. Jews who tried to offer sacrifice to God, practice
circumcision or observe the Sabbath or feast days were put
to death. The Old Testament was ordered destroyed. A
pagan altar was erected over the altar of God, and the
Temple was rededicated to Zeus. This was the "abomination
of desolation" that was caused by Antiochus (v. 31) (1, 2
Macc.).

Those apostate Jews who already had deserted the worship of God were flattered by Antiochus into completely perverting the faith of Israel. In order to remain high priest, Menelaus turned to the service of Zeus. But those Jews who knew God personally through faith took a strong stand for Him and acted in obedience to God's covenant with Israel (v. 32) (1 Macc. 1:62-63).[40]

Mattathias Maccabeus, a priest of God, and his five sons refused to forsake the covenant of God. They understood the issues of the day and could distinguish clearly between the truth of God and the errors of Hellenism. Mattathias refused to offer the pagan sacrifice and killed Antiochus' representative who ordered him to offer it. He and his sons forsook their personal possessions and fled to the mountains. Through this example they gave many others understanding of the issues of the day. Others joined them in their revolt against Antiochus' repressive measures. This was the beginning of the Maccabean revolt (1 Macc. 2:1-30). These people paid a high price. Many of them were killed and abused by Syrian forces (v. 33) (1 Macc. 2:31-38).

From time to time small groups of men joined the Maccabees to help them in their revolt against the Syrian oppression (1 Macc. 2:42-43). Many uncommitted Jews sided in with the Maccabees hypocritically for expediency sake. They did this when they saw the Maccabees winning and in order to escape the furious punishment that the Maccabees brought upon the apostate Jews (v. 34) (1 Macc. 2:44; 3:5, 8).

Several of Mattathias Maccabeus' sons were killed while leading the people of Israel who remained faithful to God's covenant (1 Macc. 9:18-21; 13:48; 16:16). Other faithful Jews suffered similar fates (1 Macc. 6:43-46; 9:26-27). God permitted these things to happen to His people so that they might be purified in order to serve Him more effectively. Christ indicated that such a refining process of God's people would go on, not only during the persecutions by Antiochus Epiphanes, but also throughout the entire end time (the word translated "until" also means *during*[41]). This refining process would continue until the time that God has appointed for it to end — the end of the end time at the second coming of Christ. Once again Daniel was reminded of two things. First, God is sovereign — He has determined the significant times of history. Second, Israel would continue to be persecuted until Christ's second coming (v. 35).

## THE CHARACTER OF THE COMING WILLFUL KING, ANTICHRIST (11:36-39)

*"Then the king will do as he pleases, and he will exalt and magnify himself above every god, and will speak monstrous things against the God of gods; and he will prosper until the indignation is finished, for that which is decreed will be done. And he will show no regard for the gods of his fathers or for the desire of women, nor will he show regard for any other god; for he will magnify himself above them all. But instead he will honor a god of fortresses, a god whom his fathers did not know; he will honor him with gold, silver, costly stones, and treasures. And he will take action against the strongest of fortresses with the help of a foreign god; he will give great honor to those who acknowledge him, and he will cause them to rule over the many, and will parcel out land for a price.*

Many scholars, both ancient and modern, Jewish and Christian, have been convinced that there is a great gap of time between the end of verse thirty-five and the beginning of verse thirty-six of Daniel 11. According to this view, the prophecies of verses two through thirty-five were filfilled by the end of the days of Antiochus Epiphanes (164 B.C.), but the prophecies beginning with verse thirty-six will be fulfilled by the Antichrist during the last several years leading up to the second coming of Christ.[42]

There are several good reasons for believing that this view is correct. First, although verses two through thirty-five have been fulfilled clearly and precisely by past historic events, there is nothing from the past that corresponds exactly with the prophecies beginning with verse thirty-six.[43] Second, other prophetic passages which describe the Antichrist correspond exactly with the description of the king beginning with verse thirty-six.[44] Third, according to Daniel 12:1, during the time of the king described in Daniel 11:36-45 "there will be a time of distress such as never occurred since there was a nation until that time." Several centuries after Christ gave this revelation to Daniel, He indicated that this unique time of distress would transpire during the time period immediately before His second coming (Mt. 24:21-22, 29-31). Jesus thereby placed the fulfillment of Daniel 11:36-12:3 into the future when Antichrist will rule.[45]

As Christ described the Antichrist, He gave insight into the character of that coming ruler. Antichrist "will do as he pleases." He will be an absolute dictator who will demand that he have his own way. He will tolerate no restraints upon himself. He will recognize no law or authority higher than himself. The Apostle Paul indicated the same character trait of the Antichrist by calling him the man of lawlessness (2 Th. 2:3). As noted earlier concerning the little horn (7:25), he will intend to alter law. He will reject all forms of established law so that he can be the law of his kingdom.

Antichrist will be a blasphemer of the true God, speaking monstrous things against Him to the point of astonishing people.[46] The same was said of him as the little horn of Daniel 7:25 and as the first beast of Revelation 13:5-6. Once he comes to power, he will be able to prosper until The Indignation is finished — until God's chastening program for Israel will be completed at the second coming of Christ (as noted earlier in Daniel 8:19). He will be able to prosper until then, because God in His sovereignty has decreed that Israel's chastening will last until then (v. 36).

Not only will Antichrist be opposed to the true God, but also he will show total disregard for the gods that his ancestors worshiped. Some have translated "gods" in the singular as *God*. Since the expression "the God of his fathers" is Jewish, they have taken this to mean that Antichrist will be a Jew. It is possible that Antichrist will be a Jew, but that cannot be concluded with certainty on the basis of this one statement. The word translated "gods" could be translated plural as well as singular, but, even if one takes it as singular, the statement "he will show no regard for the god of his fathers" could apply to any person whose ancestors were religious.

The Antichrist will show no regard for "the desire of women." Some have taken this to mean that he will not experience the normal physical desires which a man experiences toward a woman. However, since this statement appears in the midst of a list of objects of worship for which Antichrist will have no regard, it seems best to assume that "the desire of women" also refers to an object of worship. In Old Testament times it was the desire of the women of Israel to be the mother of the Messiah. In light of this, it would appear that Daniel was being told that Antichrist will have no regard for the Messiah. Not only will he refuse to worship Messiah, but also he will be totally opposed to Him. This is why the Scriptures call him Antichrist (anti Messiah) (1 Jn. 2:18, 22).

Not only will Antichrist reject the true God, the gods of his fathers and the Messiah, but also he will not show regard for any god. The Apostle Paul said that he would oppose "every so-called god or object of worship" (2 Th. 2:4). Thus, Antichrist will be an atheist — a rejecter of every form of established worship (v. 37).

Antichrist will have a specific reason for his total atheism.

According to verses thirty-six and thirty-seven he will "exalt and magnify himself above every god." He will oppose every form of established worship in order to clear the way for the worship of himself. As noted earlier, the angel who described Antichrist as the little horn declared that he would claim deity for himself and would try to speak with the same authority with which God speaks (7:25). Paul wrote that Antichrist would exalt "himself above every so-called god or object of worship, so that he takes his seat in the temple of God, displaying himself as being God" (2 Th. 2:4). John indicated that this man would be worshiped by many people (Rev. 13:4, 8, 12, 15). Jesus taught that Antichrist would erect an image of himself in the future Temple of Jerusalem — the place where God is supposed to dwell (Mt. 24:15). In other words, Antichrist will be the ultimate man — the man who supposedly achieves deity.

Although Antichrist himself will refuse to worship a personal being as god, he will honor an impersonal god. That to which a man devotes himself, his abilities, his efforts, his time and his resources is the god of that man. In place of a personal god, Antichrist will make war his god.[47] He will be devoted to the conquest of the world. Although the ancient Romans carried on extensive wars, they never deified war. They worshiped personal gods which they themselves invented. Unlike his predecessors, this future Roman ruler will deify war. Antichrist will honor his god by pouring huge sums of wealth into the building of his military machine and the waging of war (v. 38).

Antichrist's devotion to war will motivate him to attack the strongest military installations. As he conquers new areas of the world for his Roman kingdom, he will reward his most avid followers in two ways. To some he will give positions of rulership over large groups of people. To others he will give gifts of choice land. In order to obtain these rewards, people will have to pay a price — the selling of their

souls in total devotion to this man who will claim to be God
(v. 39).

# THE MILITARY CAREER AND JUDGMENT
# OF ANTICHRIST (11:40-45)

> *"And at the end time the king of the South will collide with him,
> and the king of the North will storm against him with chariots,
> with horsemen, and with many ships; and he will enter countries,
> overflow them, and pass through. He will also enter the
> Beautiful Land, and many countries will fall; but these will be
> rescued out of his hand: Edom, Moab and the foremost of the
> sons of Ammon. Then he will stretch out his hand against other
> countries, and the land of Egypt will not escape. But he will gain
> control over the hidden treasures of gold and silver, and over all
> the precious things of Egypt; and Libyans and Ethiopians will
> follow at his heels. But rumors from the East and from the North
> will disturb him, and he will go forth with great wrath to destroy
> and annihilate many. And he will pitch the tents of his royal
> pavilion between the seas and the beautiful Holy Mountain; yet
> he will come to his end, and no one will help him.*

The revelation given by Christ to Daniel in verse forty
contains some problems of interpretation. First, who is the
person referred to by *him* and *he*? Inasmuch as the
Antichrist, the future ruler of the Revived Roman Empire,
was the major subject of the immediately preceding context
(vv. 36-39), it seems rather obvious that the *him* and *he* of
verse forty refer to the Antichrist. Second, who are the king
of the South and the king of the North? As noted earlier,
these two kings were mentioned several times in Daniel 11:2-
35. Since those verses have been fulfilled already, it is a
known fact that historically the king of the South was
always Egypt and the king of the North was always Syria.
Inasmuch as Christ did not tell Daniel that the king of the
South and the king of the North of verse forty are different
from those of verses two through thirty-five, it would appear
that Christ intended them to be understood as being the

same. This would mean, then, that in verse forty the king of the South is still Egypt, and the king of the North is still Syria.

In light of these interpretations, it can be concluded that Christ revealed the following in Daniel 11:40: sometime in the end time (the word translated "at" also means *in*[48]) Egypt and Syria will attack the Antichrist militarily. When in the end time will they conduct this joint attack? Evidence will be seen later for concluding that this attack will take place during the first half of the seventieth seven of Daniel 9 (during the first half of the last seven years before Christ's second coming).

How will Egypt and Syria in the Middle East be able to attack Antichrist who will be in the West (with headquarters in Rome)? The proposed answer is as follows: in Daniel 9:27 it was noted that Antichrist will make a strong covenant with Israel at the beginning of the seventieth seven of years. That covenant will bind Israel so strongly to Antichrist that that nation will practically be an extension of this Roman ruler in the Middle East. As a result, Antichrist will regard any attack upon Israel as an attack upon himself. Through that covenant he will commit himself and his western Roman army to the military protection of Israel. In light of that binding covenant, it is proposed that the way in which Egypt and Syria will storm against the Antichrist will be through their attacking his Middle Eastern ally, Israel, in a joint invasion from the south and north.

When Antichrist learns that Israel has been attacked by Egypt and Syria, he will appear to keep his covenant. He will rush his western army to the Middle East and will invade, overrun and pass through different nations there (v. 40).

A reading of Daniel 11:41-43 indicates that Antichrist's initial military movement in the Middle East will be from the north to the south. Apparently he will conquer Syria first (north of Israel). Then he will march south through

Israel ("the Beautiful Land" — as noted earlier in 8:9 and 11:16). Many people of different countries will become subject to him, but the people of Edom and Moab and some of Ammon will escape his conquest. It appears that Antichrist will be so anxious to conquer Egypt that as he moves south, he will bypass (at least temporarily) these people who will be directly east of Israel (across the Jordan) (v. 41).

Antichrist will get his Roman army to Egypt. There he will enjoy further military success. He will rob Egypt of its wealth and will conquer to the eastern border of Libya and the northern border of Ethiopia (vv. 42-43). Apparently Antichrist will not conquer Libya and Ethiopia, because, when he will turn himself around to head north (v. 44), those two nations will be "at his heels" (behind him).

While Antichrist will be enjoying success in Egypt, he will receive disturbing news from the east and north. Since Christ did not reveal the content of that news, the most one can do is conjecture concerning that content. The predicted reaction of Antichrist to the news seems to indicate that it will inform him of new military action against him — military action from the east and north. It is proposed that the disturbing news will be that the invasion of the Middle East foretold in Ezekiel 38-39 has begun to take place. In that Ezekiel passage God revealed that Russia (the land of Magog) will lead a massive military invasion against Israel. Russia and some of its allies will come from the north (Ezek. 38:6, 15; 39:2). One of Russia's allies (Iran — ancient Persia) will send troops from the east (Ezek. 38:5). This invasion is to take place after a restoration of Israel to its homeland and when Israel will feel secure (Ezek. 38:8, 11-14). There will be only one period of time between Israel's restoration to the homeland in 1948 and the second coming of Christ when Israel will feel secure. That time will be the first three and one-half years of the seventieth seven of years. Israel will feel secure then because of the covenant that Antichrist will make with it at the beginning of the seventieth seven of years. The secure feeling will last only during the first half of the seventieth seven, because, as noted in Daniel 9:27, Antichrist himself will try to destroy Israel during the second half of those seven years. It would appear, then, that it will be during the first half of the seventieth seven of years (the first half of the future Tribulation Period) that Russia and her allies will invade Israel and that Antichrist will hear the news of that invasion while in Egypt.

When Antichrist hears that Israel has been invaded by Russia and her allies, "he will go forth with great wrath to destroy and annihilate many." He will be furious. He will turn about and rush north to Israel with the goal of annihilating the invading troops (v. 44). However, before Antichrist will arrive there, the forces of Russia and her allies will already have been destroyed by God through His divine intervention on behalf of Israel (Ezek. 38:18-39:8).

By the time Antichrist will reach Israel, the military force of his major opponent will  have been removed. This will give him a free hand to do what he wants to do in the Middle East. As a result, he will establish his royal headquarters on Mount Zion (literally, *at the glorious holy mountain* — the mountain where Jerusalem and the Temple stand[49]) between the Mediterranean and Dead Seas. Perhaps Antichrist will decide to make Jerusalem the world head-quarters of his Roman Empire, since Israel occupies the most strategic geographical location on earth — the crossroads of three major continents at the navel of the earth.

It will be obvious to all that the invading force of Russia and her allies was destroyed supernaturally. It may be that Antichrist will claim he caused that supernatural destruc-tion. As noted earlier, in the middle of the seventieth seven of years he will claim to be God and will erect an image of

himself in the rebuilt Temple in Jerusalem (where God is
supposed to dwell). Perhaps he will use the divine destruction of the invading force as his opportunity to make his
claim of deity and to give credibility to that claim. At the
time of that claim he will break his covenant with Israel and
will persecute the Jews mercilessly for the second three and
one-half years of the seventieth seven of years.

Antichrist will not be able to persecute indefinitely. In
spite of the fact that he will be energized supernaturally by
Satan and will have great power (2 Th. 2:9), "he will come to
his end, and no one will help him" (v. 45). As noted earlier,
he will be judged so thoroughly by God through Jesus Christ
at the second coming that no one will be able to deliver or
help him (Dan. 7:11-14, 25-26; 2 Th. 2:8; Rev. 19:11-21). He
will be cast into the Lake of Fire where he will be under
divine judgment forever (Rev. 20:10).

## GOD'S FINAL DELIVERANCE
## OF ISRAEL (12:1-3)

*"Now at that time Michael, the great prince who stands guard
over the sons of your people, will arise. And there will be a time
of distress such as never occurred since there was a nation until
that time; and at that time your people, everyone who is found
written in the book, will be rescued. And many of those who
sleep in the dust of the ground will awake, these to everlasting
life, but the others to disgrace and everlasting contempt. And
those who have insight will shine brightly like the brightness of
the expanse of heaven, and those who lead the many to
righteousness, like the stars forever and ever.*

Christ began the conclusion of this new revelation to
Daniel by stating, "Now at that time . . . ." To what time was
He referring? Inasmuch as the last time reference was "the
end time" in Daniel 11:40, it is rather obvious that Christ
was referring to the time when the events of Daniel 11:40-45
will take place.[50] Thus, Christ was saying the following:

when Egypt and Syria will attack Antichrist by invading Israel during the first half of the seventieth seven of years, Michael, the great angelic prince whom God has assigned to protect Israel, will stand up to guard that nation (cf. Dan. 10:21).

Why will Michael stand up to protect Israel at that time? The reason is this: Israel's invasion by Egypt and Syria will begin a chain of events that will bring great suffering to the Jews. First will be the joint invasion by Egypt and Syria. Second, Antichrist will march his Roman army through Israel. Third, Russia and her allies will launch a massive military attack against Israel. Fourth, Antichrist will break his covenant with Israel and will persecute the Jews horribly.

All four links of this future chain of events will hurt Israel, but the fourth link will bring the worst suffering. When Antichrist will begin his persecution of the Jews in the middle of the seventieth seven of years, Israel will experience "a time of distress such as never occurred since there was a nation until that time." Satan will do everything in his power to annihilate the nation of Israel from the earth during the second half of the seventieth seven of years (Rev. 12:13-17). Moses talked about this distress for Israel in the latter days (Dt. 4:30). Jeremiah called it "the time of Jacob's distress" (Jer. 30:7). Jesus Christ said concerning this distress: "then there will be a great tribulation, such as has not occurred since the beginning of the world until now, nor ever shall, and unless those days had been cut short, no life would have been saved" (Mt. 24:21-22). He warned that the Jews of that time should flee to hiding places (Mt. 24:15-20). Two-thirds of the Jews will lose their lives during those three and one-half years (Zech. 13:8). This will be far worse than the Holocaust of World War II. How necessary it will be for Michael to stand up to guard Israel from total annihilation!

God in His sovereignty will not permit Israel to be totally

obliterated from the earth. Through His supernatural intervention He will preserve a remnant consisting of one-third of the Jews (Jer. 30:7, 11; Zech. 13:8; Mt. 24:22; Rev. 12:6, 14-16). Although God will preserve the lives of one-third of the Jews, He will allow that remnant to suffer severe persecutions — this will be His way of refining out their rebellious unbelief to the point that they will believe in Jesus as their Messiah and Savior (Dt. 4:30-31; Zech. 13:9). When Jesus Christ will return to end Israel's great time of distress, the great majority of Jews of the one-third remnant will believe in Him whom their nation had pierced (Zech. 12:10-14). They will be cleansed from their sin (Zech. 13:1). At that time (the second coming of Christ) those saved Jews (whose names will be found written in the book of life) will be rescued by Christ from the great distress (v. 1). Christ will end the time of great distress, will purge out from the remnant any minority of Jews who still refuse to believe in Him (Ezek. 20:33-38) and will send the saved Jews into the Millennial Kingdom of God. Thus, all of Israel left on the earth to enter the future Kingdom of God will be saved (Rom. 11:25-31).

Is it only the Jews who will be alive and saved at the second coming who will enter the Millennial Kingdom of God to enjoy its blessings? What will happen to those Jews who were saved and died during the seventieth seven of years and Old Testament times? Christ gave revelation answering these questions in Daniel 12:2. There He referred to bodily resurrection from the dead: "And many of those who sleep in the dust of the ground will awake." The fact that Christ said "many" rather than *all* indicates that He was not teaching a general resurrection of all the dead at the same time.[51] The Bible teaches that there are different orders of resurrection, separated from each other by time (1 Cor. 15:20-24). It would appear, then, that Christ was saying that many will be resurrected at one time, but others will be resurrected at another time. It is obvious that the many who will be resurrected at one time died as believers, for they will be resurrected "to everlasting life." The others who will be resurrected at another time died as unbelievers, for they will be resurrected "to disgrace and everlasting contempt." When will these different orders of resurrection take place? Revelation 20:4-6, 11-15 gives the answer. That passage teaches that the resurrection of those who will get saved and die during the seventieth seven of years will take place at the second coming of Christ. These Tribulation saints will be resurrected to enter the Millennial Kingdom of God with Christ (later it will be seen from Daniel 12:13 that Old Testament saints will also be resurrected at this time). Revelation 20 also teaches that all the unsaved of all ages of time will be resurrected at the Great White Throne Judgment after the Millennium has been completed. Thus, Christ was revealing to Daniel that Jews who were saved and died during the seventieth seven of years and Old Testament times will be resurrected at the second coming of Christ to take part in the blessings of the Millennial Kingdom of God (v. 2).

Some people of the coming Tribulation Period will have enough insight into the lies of Antichrist and the truth of God to reject and oppose Antichrist and to believe in Christ unto salvation. They also will lead many other people away from Antichrist and to Christ ("to righteousness"). They will do this while facing the horrors of persecution by Antichrist. Thus, their activity will be similar to that of the Maccabeans during the persecutions by Antiochus Epiphanes (Dan. 11:33, 35). These Tribulation saints will be rewarded for their service. They will be given the capacity to shine forth the glory of God forever, just as the present expanse of heaven shines forth that glory through its luminous bodies (v. 3) (Ps. 19:1; Mt. 13:43).[52]

At this point Christ's new revelation to Daniel ended. It

was designed to show how God would sovereignly chasten yet preserve Israel as a nation both in the near future (through the reign of Antiochus Epiphanes) and in the far future (during the reign of Antichrist).

# 12

## FINAL INSTRUCTIONS
## AND QUESTIONS
## Chapter 12:4-13

### THE COMMAND TO PRESERVE
### THE REVELATION (12:4)

*"But as for you, Daniel, conceal these words and seal up the
book until the end of time; many will go back and forth, and
knowledge will increase."*

After Christ finished giving the new revelation to Daniel,
He commanded him to preserve "these words" (the new
revelation from 11:2 through 12:3) and "the book" (perhaps
the entire Book of Daniel) for the duration of the end time
(the word translated "until" also means *during* as noted in
Daniel 11:35). The word translated "conceal" refers to a
preservation of the revelation (the same word had the same
meaning in Daniel 8:26).[1] The word translated "seal up"
carries the same meaning.[2]

Christ gave the reason for the preservation of the new
revelation and the Book of Daniel. Throughout the entire
end time (530's B.C. to the second coming) many people
would run to and fro in their effort to gain knowledge about
the future. As a result of the revelations given to Daniel
being preserved for the duration of the end time, these
people would be able to study it and thereby increase their
knowledge of the future.[3]

There is a lesson to be learned from these words of Christ.
Instead of running to and fro to psychics, so-called modern-
day prophets and speculators, people should turn to the

written Scriptures to obtain knowledge about the future. They are the reliable authoritative source of information on the subject, for their ultimate source is the sovereign God who has determined what will happen, who rules over the entire course of history and who knows the end from the beginning.

## AN ANGEL'S QUESTION (12:5-7)

*Then I, Daniel, looked and behold, two others were standing, one on this bank of the river, and the other on that bank of the river. And one said to the man dressed in linen, who was above the waters of the river, "How long will it be until the end of these wonders?" And I heard the man dressed in linen, who was above the waters of the river, as he raised his right hand and his left toward heaven, and swore by Him who lives forever that it would be for a time, times, and half a time; and as soon as they finish shattering the power of the holy people, all these events will be completed.*

While Christ was talking with Daniel, two angels appeared suddenly on the banks of the Tigris River (cf. Dan. 10:4). It may be that they had been present for some time in their invisible state before making themselves visible to Daniel, for it is apparent that they had heard at least part of the new revelation delivered by Christ (v. 5). One of these angels asked Christ (cf. Dan. 10:5) the following question: "until how long is the end of wondrous things?"[4] The angel was not asking how long all the wondrous things of Daniel 11:40-12:3 will continue. Instead, he was asking how long "the end" of those wondrous things will continue. In other words, he wanted to know how long the Antichrist will be able to continue his persecution of Israel once he breaks his covenant with that nation (v. 6).[5]

In response to the angel's question, Christ raised both hands toward heaven and swore an oath by God. Usually only one hand is raised in the swearing of an oath. The fact that Christ raised both hands emphasized the solemnity and importance of the oath.[6] Since Christ put His answer in the form of an oath, and since He based this oath on the eternal God who is sovereign and truthful, it is obvious that He was asserting the truthfulness and reliability of His answer in the strongest way possible.

Christ's answer to the angel's question was twofold. First, He swore that Antichrist will be able to persecute Israel "for a time, times, and half a time." As already noted from other passages, this amounts to three and one-half years (Dan. 7:25; Rev. 11:2; 12:6, 14; 13:5). It will be the latter three and one-half years of the seventieth seven of years (Tribulation Period). Second, Christ indicated that Antichrist's persecutions of Israel will be completed as soon as the shattering of Israel's stubborn rebellion has been finished. As noted earlier, Israel's rebellion against God will stop at the end of the seventieth seven of years at the second coming of Christ. At that time Israel will believe in Christ. In other words, Christ was promising with a solemn oath that Antichrist's oppression of Israel will last only until it accomplishes its sovereignly designed purpose — the conversion of Israel (v. 7).

# DANIEL'S QUESTIONS (12:8-13)

*As for me, I heard but could not understand; so I said, "My lord, what will be the outcome of these events?" And he said, "Go your way, Daniel, for these words are concealed and sealed up until the end time. Many will be purged, purified and refined; but the wicked will act wickedly, and none of the wicked will understand, but those who have insight will understand. And from the time that the regular sacrifice is abolished, and the abomination of desolation is set up, there will be 1290 days. How blessed is he who keeps waiting and attains to the 1335 days! But as for you, go your way to the end; then you will enter into rest and rise again for your allotted portion at the end of the age."*

Daniel had heard the revelation and Christ's answer to the angel's question, but there were things about the revelation that he still was not understanding. In his desire to gain more understanding, Daniel asked Christ the following question: "My lord, what will be the outcome of these events?" Daniel's question differed in two ways from the question asked by the angel in verse six. First, Daniel asked "what" instead of "how long."[7] He was requesting an explanation or event, not a length of time. Second, the word used by Daniel for "outcome" was different from the word used by the angel for "end" in verse six. Daniel's word referred to the *last part* or *closing stage* of events.[8] Thus, Daniel, was asking, not about all the events related to Antichrist's persecution of Israel, but about the last event related to that persecution — namely, the final deliverance of Israel as foretold by Christ in Daniel 12:1. Daniel wanted an explanation of how that deliverance will be accomplished.[9] As an Israelite who loved his nation, he was intensely interested in that (v. 8).

Christ refused to give Daniel any further explanation. He commanded him to go on in life without further inquiry. Christ gave the following reason for that command: "for these words are concealed and sealed up until the end time." As noted in verse four where the same terms were used, this meant that the revelation was preserved for the duration of the end time. The purpose for preserving something for the duration of a period of time is that it might have significance at the end of that time. Christ's point, then, was this: Daniel should not be concerned any further about the revelation of the final end of these events, because it would not be significant to him. There was no need for him to know all the details, for the revelation would not be fulfilled while he lived. It will be significant to those who will live during its fulfillment at the end of the end time. This preserved revelation will help them and give them insight into the events of their day (v. 9).[10] Thus, the revelation was not given primarily for his benefit.

Christ indicated that many Jews will get saved during the latter half of the seventieth seven of years. Antichrist's persecuting activity will purge out their rebellion and prompt them to turn to Christ. But the rest of the Jews will be characterized by wickedness — they will continue in their wickedness. Those who get saved during that time will understand the revelation that was given to Daniel, but the wicked Jews of that time will not understand it (v. 10).[11]

In verses eleven and twelve Christ referred to two different amounts of future days — 1,290 days and 1,335 days. Both sets of days will begin at the same time — the middle of the seventieth seven of years when Antichrist will end the regular sacrifices at the Temple and will set up his image in that holy place. Since the latter half of the seventieth seven of years will consist of 1,260 days, both of these sets of days will extend beyond the end of the Tribulation Period and second coming of Christ. The 1,290 days will go thirty days beyond; the 1,335 days will extend to seventy-five days beyond.

Christ did not give the significance of these two sets of days, but the fact that He referred to them seems to indicate that they will end on the dates of important events. At this time only an educated guess can be made concerning what those important events will be. First, it may be that the 1,290 days will end on the day that will conclude the judgments to take place after the second coming. The Scriptures teach that Christ will judge Israel and the Gentiles (the people who will survive the Tribulation Period alive) after His return and before the establishment of the Millennial Kingdom of God (Ezek. 20:34-38; Mt. 25:31-46) The purpose of this judgment will be to separate the believers and unbelievers, so that the believers can enter the Millennial Kingdom of God and the unbelievers can be removed from the earth in judgment. It may take thirty days after the second coming of Christ to finish these judgments.[12]

Second, perhaps the 1,335 days will end on the day that will begin the Millennial Kingdom of God. Once the judgments determining who can enter that kingdom have been concluded, it may take another forty-five days to form the government structure necessary to operate the kingdom.[13] The Scriptures indicate that the saints will reign with Christ in the Millennial Kingdom (Rev. 20:4-6). After the saints and unbelievers have been separated, it will take time to appoint saints to different government posts and to inform them of their various responsibilities.

Christ said: "How blessed is he who keeps waiting and attains to the 1335 days!" In light of this strong statement, it is apparent that whatever will happen or begin on the 1,335th day is both "good and desirable."[14] The word translated "he who keeps waiting" means *one who waits earnestly*.[15] Certainly the Tribulation saints will wait earnestly for the Kingdom of God to come as they face the horrors of the war that Antichrist will wage against them. As a result of the preserved revelation of the Book of Daniel, they will understand that, once the Kingdom of God begins, never again will they be threatened by the terrors produced by man's attempt to rule the earth apart from God.

The sets of 1,290 and 1,335 days are significant for at least two other reasons. First, they indicated that some Jews will survive God's chastening program and will enter the Millennial Kingdom of God to enjoy its blessings. This would have reassured Daniel that, in spite of the horrors of the future, a remnant of Israel would be preserved. The nation would survive. Second, the fact that these sets of days will extend beyond the seventieth seven of years and second coming indicates that time will not end and the future eternal state will not begin at the second coming of Christ. The twenty-four hour day cycle of the solar system and the history of the earth will continue after the Lord's return (vv. 11-12).

Once again Christ commanded Daniel to go on in life without further inquiry until he died. The Lord clearly indicated that he would die ("will enter into rest"), but He also declared that Daniel would be resurrected from the dead. The time of Daniel's resurrection would be "at the end of the days."[16] This meant that Daniel would take part in the resurrection of believers at the second coming of Christ at the end of the days of the seventieth seven of years — the resurrection which Christ had foretold in Daniel 12:2.[17] Since Daniel was an Old Testament saint, this would seem to imply that the resurrection of Old Testament saints will take place at the second coming of Christ at the end of the Tribulation Period.[18]

Christ told Daniel that he would be resurrected for his "allotted portion" ("to receive his inheritance lot").[19] Since he will be resurrected at the second coming, certainly part of his inheritance lot will be to enter and enjoy the blessings of the future Kingdom of God which God had made known to him in chapters two and seven (v. 13). In light of the clear demonstration of God's sovereign rule over kingdoms, events and persons witnessed by Daniel during his lifetime, he had every reason to believe that these personal promises to him would be fulfilled.

# CONCLUSION

The Book of Daniel clearly demonstrates the sovereign rule of God over the realm of mankind. The study of this book has shown that God has fulfilled numerous prophecies with exact precision. Gentile world dominion has run the exact course that God said it would. Israel has continued to be chastened and yet preserved by God, just as He promised. Messiah did present Himself as Prince to Israel in April, 32 A.D., and was put to death after that presentation, precisely as God foretold. Jerusalem and the Temple were destroyed by the Romans after the presentation and death of Messiah as predicted.

These fulfilled prophecies not only demonstrate the sovereignty of God, but also guarantee the fulfillment of prophecies concerning the future. The Roman Empire will be revived as a ten nation confederation. An ultimate man, Antichrist, will rule that empire as an absolute dictator. There will be a time of unprecedented distress for the world. Israel will experience its worst period of suffering. Messiah will return in a second coming to judge Antichrist and Gentile world dominion. A remnant of Israel will be rescued from destruction and will repent and believe in Jesus Christ at His second coming. The Kingdom of God will be established on earth. Believers will enter the Kingdom of God to enjoy its blessings. Just as the prophecies concerning events of the past were fulfilled, so these prophecies concerning events of the future are certain to be fulfilled.

Modern-day events take on added significance in light of the Book of Daniel. The prophecies of that book implied that Israel would be in its homeland as a nation in time for the events of the seventieth seven of years (the Tribulation Period). Israel was restored to its homeland as a nation in 1948. Leaders of Europe do meet to discuss the formation of a confederation of nations. Egypt and Syria have already invaded Israel militarily (a foretaste of their future attack in the seventieth seven of years). Humanists talk about man achieving divinity. Only God knows when the prophecies of the future in Daniel will be fulfilled, but current trends may indicate that the world is hurtling rapidly toward that time.

In light of the precise fulfillment of prophecies about the past, the certainty of the fulfillment of prophecies about the future and the ominous direction of the present, two things are most urgent. First, it is imperative that individual unbelievers admit that they cannot win against the sovereignty of God. They must recognize that their going their own way to live their lives the way they please and their failure to accept God's way of salvation are individual expressions of man's rebellion against the rule of God. They must concede the fact that there is only one way of salvation for them (Jn. 14:6) and that God has provided that one way by sending His Son, the Messiah, to die for their sins, to be buried and to be resurrected on the third day after His death (1 Cor. 15:1-4). Having come to this point, it is essential that they trust Jesus, the Messiah, totally to save them from the penalty of their sins (Jn. 3:16; 1:11-13; Acts 16:30-31). Any attempt on their part to save themselves by their own works rather than by the sovereign grace of God will be another expression of man's rebellious attempt to solve his own problems apart from God (Gal. 3:9-11; Eph. 2:8-9; Ti. 3:5-7). Failure to come to God His way will result in certain eternal judgment under the wrath of the sovereign God (Mt.

13:40-42, 49-50; 25:41, 46; Rev. 20:11-15). Reader, have you personally trusted Jesus, the Messiah, as your Savior from sin?

Second, it is imperative that believers personally saturate themselves with the truth of the sovereignty of God, commit their lives to that truth and allow it to affect their lives as it affected Daniel's. It gave Daniel stability and purpose in times of personal and world upheaval and crisis. It gave him boldness and courage to live a godly life and to refuse to compromise the truth of God in a pagan world that tried to humiliate the true God and to pressure him into conformity with it. It provided him with insight and understanding which his pagan contemporaries never had. These are qualities God's people need today in the midst of a world that becomes increasingly unstable and irritated with the idea of God and the restraints of His rule.

# NOTES ON SOURCES

## Chapter 1

[1] Samuel J. Schultz, *The Old Testament Speaks* (New York: Harper & Brothers, Publishers, 1960), pp. 233-34.

[2] *Ibid.*, p. 234.

[3] *Ibid.*

[4] *Ibid.*

[5] Charles Boutflower, *In And Around The Book Of Daniel* (Grand Rapids: Zondervan Publishing House, 1963), pp. 93, 133.

[6] C. F. Keil, *Biblical Commentary On The Book Of Daniel* (Grand Rapids: Wm. B. Eerdmans Publishing Company, 1959), p. 73.

[7] Boutflower, *In And Around The Book Of Daniel,* pp. 35-36.

[8] T. G. Pinches, "Chaldea, Chaldeans," *The International Standard Bible Encyclopedia,* general editor, James Orr (5 vols.: Grand Rapids: Wm. B. Eerdmans Publishing Company, 1957), I, 591.

[9] Edward J. Young, *The Prophecy Of Daniel* (Grand Rapids: Wm. B. Eerdmans Publishing Company, 1970), p. 42.

[10] John F. Walvoord, *Daniel* (Chicago: Moody Press, 1971), p. 36.

[11] *Ibid.*, pp. 36-37.

[12] Young, *The Prophecy Of Daniel,* p. 44.

## Chapter 2

[1] H. C. Leupold, *Exposition Of Daniel* (Grand Rapids: Baker Book House, 1949), pp. 29-30.

[2] Charles Boutflower, *In And Around The Book Of Daniel* (Grand Rapids: Zondervan Publishing House, 1963), p. xv.

[3] Edward J. Young, *The Prophecy of Daniel* (Grand Rapids: Wm. B. Eerdmans Publishing Company, 1970), pp. 58-60.

[4] Leupold, *Exposition Of Daniel,* pp. 89-90.

[5] Boutflower, *In And Around The Book Of Daniel,* p. 47.

[6] Young, *The Prophecy Of Daniel,* p. 74.

[7] Boutflower, *In And Around The Book Of Daniel,* p. 34.

[8] *Ibid.*, pp. 25-26.

[9] Leupold, *Exposition Of Daniel,* p. 117.

[10] Boutflower, *In And Around The Book Of Daniel,* pp. 26-28.

[11] C. F. Keil, *Biblical Commentary On The Book Of Daniel* (Grand Rapids: Wm. B. Eerdmans Publishing Company, 1959), p. 106.

[12] Boutflower, *In And Around The Book Of Daniel,* p. xvi.

[13] Leupold, *Exposition Of Daniel,* p. 118.

[14] Boutflower, *In And Around The Book Of Daniel*, pp. 29-30.
[15] Samuel J. Schultz, *The Old Testament Speaks* (New York: Harper & Brothers, Publishers, 1960), p. 248.
[16] John F. Walvoord, *Daniel* (Chicago: Moody Press, 1971), p. 73.
[17] Boutflower, *In And Around The Book Of Daniel*, pp. 31-32.
[18] *Ibid.*, p. 45.
[19] *Ibid.*
[20] *Ibid.*, p. 46.
[21] *Ibid.*, pp. 47-48.
[22] *Ibid.*, pp. 46-47.
[23] *Ibid.*, p. 25.
[24] *Ibid.*

## Chapter 3

[1] Edward J. Young, *The Prophecy Of Daniel* (Grand Rapids: Wm. B. Eerdmans Publishing Company, 1970), p. 85.
[2] *Ibid.*
[3] *Ibid.*
[4] *Ibid.*, p. 90.
[5] *Ibid.*, p. 88.
[6] H. C. Leupold, *Exposition Of Daniel* (Grand Rapids: Baker Book House, 1949), p. 154.
[7] *Ibid.*, p. 157.
[8] *Ibid.*, p. 158.
[9] Young, *The Prophecy Of Daniel*, p. 94.
[10] Leon Wood, *A Commentary On Daniel* (Grand Rapids: Zondervan Publishing House, 1973), p. 93.

## Chapter 4

[1] Charles Boutflower, *In And Around The Book Of Daniel* (Grand Rapids: Zondervan Publishing House, 1963), p. 104.
[2] *Ibid.*
[3] H. C. Leupold, *Exposition Of Daniel* (Grand Rapids: Baker Book House, 1949), p. 172.
[4] Edward J. Young, *The Prophecy Of Daniel* (Grand Rapids: Wm. B. Eerdmans Publishing Company, 1970), p. 103.
[5] Boutflower, *In And Around The Book Of Daniel*, p. 37.
[6] *Ibid.*, p. 90.
[7] *Ibid.*, p. 91.
[8] *Ibid.*, p. 79.
[9] *Ibid.*, pp. 79-80.
[10] *Ibid.*, p. 83.
[11] *Ibid.*, pp. 83-84.
[12] *Ibid.*, pp. 66-68.

[13] *Ibid.*, p. 68.

[14] *Ibid.*, p. 69.

[15] Will Durant, *Our Oriental Heritage* (New York: Simon and Schuster, 1954), p. 224.

[16] Boutflower, *In And Around The Book Of Daniel,* p. 68.

[17] *Ibid.*, pp. 71, 74-75.

[18] *Ibid.*, p. 71.

[19] Young, *The Prophecy Of Daniel*, p. 109.

[20] Leon Wood, *A Commentary On Daniel* (Grand Rapids: Zondervan Publishing House, 1973), p. 119.

[21] Boutflower, *In And Around The Book Of Daniel,* p. 71.

[22] *Ibid.*, p. 76.

[23] *Ibid.*, pp. 66-68.

[24] Durant, *Our Oriental Heritage*, p. 225.

[25] Boutflower, *In And Around The Book Of Daniel,* p. 97.

[26] Young, *The Prophecy Of Daniel*, p. 112.

[27] *Ibid.*

[28] Boutflower, *In And Around The Book Of Daniel*, pp. 105-06.

[29] *Ibid.*

[30] *Ibid.*, pp. 30, 111-12.

[31] Durant, *Our Oriental Heritage*, p. 263.

# Chapter 5

[1] A. T. Olmstead, *History Of The Persian Empire* (Chicago: The University of Chicago Press, 1959), p. 35.

[2] Edward J. Young, *The Prophecy Of Daniel* (Grand Rapids: Wm. B. Eerdmans Publishing Company, 1970), p. 298.

[3] *Ibid.*, p. 115.

[4] Olmstead, *History Of The Persian Empire*, p. 37.

[5] *Ibid.*, p. 38.

[6] *Ibid.*

[7] Young, *The Prophecy Of Daniel*, pp. 118-19.

[8] *Ibid.*, p. 119.

[9] Charles Boutflower, *In And Around The Book Of Daniel* (Grand Rapids: Zondervan Publishing House, 1963), p. 117.

[10] Young, *The Prophecy of Daniel*, p. 119.

[11] Boutflower, *In And Around The Book Of Daniel*, pp. 114-15.

[12] *Ibid.*, pp. 121-132.

[13] Olmstead, *History Of The Persian Empire*, p. 39.

[14] *Ibid.*, p. 35.

[15] Boutflower, *In And Around The Book Of Daniel*, pp. 122-23.

[16] *Ibid.*, pp. 122, 124.

[17] *Ibid.*

[18] Young, *The Prophecy Of Daniel*, p. 121.

[19] *Ibid.*

[20] Boutflower, *In And Around The Book Of Daniel*, pp. 116-17.

[21] Leon Wood, *A Commentary On Daniel* (Grand Rapids: Zondervan Publishing House, 1973), p. 149.

[22] *Ibid.*

[23] *Ibid.*

[24] Young, *The Prophecy Of Daniel*, p. 125.

[25] Wood, *A Commentary On Daniel*, p. 149.

[26] *Ibid.*, p. 150.

[27] *Ibid.*

[28] Boutflower, *In And Around The Book Of Daniel*, pp. 138-39.

[29] *Ibid.*, pp. 122-25.

[30] *Ibid.*, pp. 124-25.

[31] Olmstead, *History Of The Persian Empire*, p. 50.

[32] Boutflower, *In And Around The Book Of Daniel*, pp. 145, 153-54.

[33] Wood, *A Commentary On Daniel*, p. 155.

[34] *Ibid.*, pp. 153-54. For a full exposition of this view see: John C. Whitcomb, *Darius the Mede* (Grand Rapids: Wm. B. Eerdmans Publishing Co., 1959).

[35] Olmstead, *History Of The Persian Empire,* p. 59.

[36] *Ibid.*

[37] *Ibid.*, p. 56.

## Chapter 6

[1] Edward J. Young, *The Prophecy Of Daniel* (Grand Rapids: Wm. B. Eerdmans Publishing Company, 1970), p. 132.

[2] *Ibid.*

[3] Will Durant, *Our Oriental Heritage* (New York: Simon and Schuster, 1954), p. 361.

[4] Young, *The Prophecy Of Daniel*, p. 136.

[5] C. F. Keil, *Biblical Commentary On The Book Of Daniel* (Grand Rapids: Wm. B. Eerdmans Publishing Company, 1959), p. 215.

[6] *Ibid.*, p. 216.

[7] Leon Wood, *A Commentary On Daniel* (Grand Rapids: Zondervan Publishing House, 1973), p. 169.

[8] Young, *The Prophecy Of Daniel*, p. 138.

## Chapter 7

[1] Leon Wood, *A Commentary On Daniel* (Grand Rapids: Zondervan Publishing House, 1973), p. 179.

[2] Edward J. Young, *The Prophecy Of Daniel* (Grand Rapids: Wm. B. Eerdmans Publishing Company, 1970), p. 143.

[3] H. C. Leupold, *Exposition Of Daniel* (Grand Rapids: Baker Book House, 1949), pp. 288-89.

[4] Wood, *A Commentary On Daniel,* p. 183.

5 Young, *The Prophecy Of Daniel*, p. 145.
6 C. E. Van Sickle, *A Political And Cultural History Of The Ancient World*, I (Chicago: Houghton Mifflin Company, 1947), p. 594.
7 *Ibid.*, p. 597.
8 Leupold, *Exposition Of Daniel*, p. 294.
9 *Ibid.*, p. 299.
10 *Ibid.*, p. 298.
11 Young, *The Prophecy Of Daniel*, p. 152.
12 Leupold, *Exposition Of Daniel*, p. 304.
13 Wood, *A Commentary On Daniel*, p. 193.
14 Young, *The Prophecy Of Daniel*, p. 160.

## Chapter 8

1 Leon Wood, *A Commentary On Daniel* (Grand Rapids: Zondervan Publishing House, 1973), p. 207.
2 *Ibid.*
3 Edward J. Young, *The Prophecy Of Daniel* (Grand Rapids: Wm. B. Eerdmans Publishing Company, 1970), p. 166.
4 *Ibid.*, p. 167.
5 Charles Boutflower, *In And Around The Book Of Daniel* (Grand Rapids: Zondervan Publishing House, 1963), p. 216.
6 Young, *The Prophecy Of Daniel*, p. 167.
7 C. F. Keil, *Biblical Commentary On The Book Of Daniel* (Grand Rapids: Wm. B. Eerdmans Publishing Company, 1959), p. 290.
8 Young, *The Prophecy Of Daniel*, p. 168.
9 C. E. Van Sickle, *A Political And Cultural History Of The Ancient World*, I (Chicago: Houghton Mifflin Company, 1947), pp. 583-590.
10 *Ibid.*, pp. 599-600.
11 Wood, *A Commentary On Daniel*, p. 212.
12 *Ibid.*
13 Young, *The Prophecy Of Daniel*, p. 170.
14 H. C. Leupold, *Exposition Of Daniel* (Grand Rapids: Baker Book House, 1949), p. 346.
15 Young, *The Prophecy Of Daniel*, 175.
16 Wood, *A Commentary On Daniel*, p. 218.
17 *Ibid.*
18 *Ibid.*, p. 222.
19 *Ibid.*, p. 226.
20 Keil, *Biblical Commentary On The Book Of Daniel*, p. 317.
21 Will Durant, *The Life Of Greece* (New York: Simon and Schuster, 1939), pp. 580-81.
22 Leupold, *Exposition Of Daniel*, p. 365.
23 Durant, *The Life Of Greece*, p. 574.
24 *Ibid.*, p. 582.
25 *Ibid.*

[26] *Ibid.*, p. 574.
[27] *Ibid.*
[28] Leupold, *Exposition Of Daniel,* pp. 370-71.

# Chapter 9

[1] Leon Wood, *Commentary On Daniel* (Grand Rapids: Zondervan Publishing House, 1973), p. 232.
[2] *Ibid.,*.p. 234.
[3] *Ibid.*, p. 236.
[4] *Ibid.*, p. 240.
[5] Edward J. Young, *The Prophecy Of Daniel* (Grand Rapids: Wm. B. Eerdmans Publishing Company, 1970), p. 190.
[6] Wood, *A Commentary On Daniel*, p. 246.
[7] H. C. Leupold, *Exposition Of Daniel* (Grand Rapids: Baker Book House, 1949), p. 412.
[8] Wood, *A Commentary On Daniel*, p. 249.
[9] *Ibid.*
[10] Leupold, *Exposition Of Daniel*, p. 414.
[11] Wood, *A Commentary On Daniel*, p. 250.
[12] *Ibid.*
[13] John C. Whitcomb, Jr., unpublished class notes, Grace Theological Seminary, Winona Lake, Indiana, 1969.
[14] James A. Montgomery, *The Book Of Daniel* (New York: Charles Scribner's Sons, 1927), p. 380.
[15] Albert Barnes, *Notes On The Book Of Daniel* (London: George Routledge & Co., 1853), p. 143.
[16] *Ibid.*, p. 139.
[17] J. Barton Payne, *The Theology Of The Older Testament* (Grand Rapids: Zondervan Publishing House, 1962), p. 277.
[18] Young, *The Prophecy Of Daniel,* p. 205.
[19] Paul Couderc, "Calendar-Year," *The Encyclopedia Americana*, 1969, V, 184.
[20] Immanuel Velikovsky, *Worlds In Collision* (New York: Dell Publishing Co., Inc., 1965), pp. 330-341.
[21] Sir Robert Anderson, *The Coming Prince* (Grand Rapids: Kregel Publications, 1954), pp. 122, 128.
[22] *Ibid.*, p. 128. For a thorough explanation of the computations involved, see Anderson, *The Coming Prince*, or Alva J. Mc Clain, *Daniel's Prophecy Of The 70 Weeks* (Grand Rapids: Zondervan Publishing House, 1978).
[23] *Ibid.*, pp. 125-27.
[24] Young, *The Prophecy Of Daniel*, p. 206.
[25] *Ibid.*, p. 207.
[26] For a study of these and other factors, see the following: Renald E. Showers, "New Testament Chronology And The Decree Of Daniel 9," *Grace Journal* (Winter, 1970), XI, pp. 30-39.

[27] *Ibid.*, pp. 31-32.

[28] W. M. Ramsay, *Luke The Physician* (New York: A. C. Armstrong and Son, 1908), pp. 227-28.

[29] Jack Finegan, *Handbook Of Biblical Chronology* (Princeton: Princeton Universtiy Press, 1964), pp. 259, 392.

[30] *Ibid.*, p. 253.

[31] *Ibid.*, p. 284.

[32] *Ibid.*, p. 253.

[33] G. Ogg, "Chronology Of The New Testament," *The New Bible Dictionary*, 1962, p. 224.

[34] S. A. Cook, F. E. Adcock and M. P. Charlesworth, ed., *The Augustan Empire, 44 B. C. - 70 A. D.*, Vol. X: *The Cambridge Ancient History* (Cambridge: The University Press, 1963), p. 331.

[35] W. Shaw Caldecott, *Herod's Temple* (London: Charles H. Kelly, n.d.), p. 15.

[36] Finegan, *Handbook Of Biblical Chronology*, p. 283.

[37] Wood, *A Commentary On Daniel*, p. 255.

[38] John F. Walvoord, *Daniel* (Chicago: Moody Press, 1971), p. 230.

[39] C. F. Keil, *Biblical Commentary On The Book Of Daniel* (Grand Rapids: Wm. B. Eerdmans Publishing Company, 1959), p. 362.

[40] *Ibid.*

[41] Young, *The Prophecy Of Daniel*, p. 207.

[42] Keil, *Biblical Commentary On The Book Of Daniel*, p. 363.

[43] *Ibid.*

[44] Wood, *A Commentary On Daniel*, p. 258.

[45] Keil, *Biblical Commentary On The Book Of Daniel*, pp. 366-67.

[46] Young, *The Prophecy Of Daniel*, p. 219.

[47] Wood, *A Commentary On Daniel*, p. 261.

[48] *Ibid.*, pp. 261, 263.

# Chapters 10:1-11:1

[1] John F. Walvoord, *Daniel* (Chicago: Moody Press, 1971), p. 238.

[2] Leon Wood, *A Commentary On Daniel* (Grand Rapids: Zondervan Publishing House, 1973), p. 265.

[3] *Ibid.*

[4] *Ibid.*, pp. 266-67.

[5] Walvoord, *Daniel*, pp. 241-42.

[6] H. C. Leupold, *Exposition Of Daniel* (Grand Rapids: Baker Book House, 1949), p. 449.

[7] Edward J. Young, *The Prophecy of Daniel* (Grand Rapids: Wm. B. Eerdmans Publishing Company, 1970), p. 225.

[8] Wood, *A Commentary On Daniel*, p. 270.

[9] Young, *The Prophecy Of Daniel*, p. 226.

[10] Wood, *A Commentary On Daniel*, p. 271.

[11] A. T. Olmstead, *History Of The Persian Empire* (Chicago: The Uni-

versity of Chicago Press, 1959), p. 57.

## Chapters 11:2-12:3

[1] John F. Walvoord, *Daniel* (Chicago: Moody Press, 1971), pp. 252-254.

[2] *Ibid.*, p. 256.

[3] *Ibid.*

[4] *Ibid.*

[5] Leon Wood, *A Commentary On Daniel* (Grand Rapids: Zondervan Publishing House, 1973), p. 281.

[6] *Ibid.*, p. 282.

[7] Will Durant, *The Life Of Greece* (New York: Simon and Schuster, 1939), p. 555.

[8] Edward J. Young, *The Prophecy Of Daniel* (Grand Rapids: Wm. B. Eerdmans Publishing Company, 1970), p. 234.

[9] Walvoord, *Daniel,* pp. 258-59.

[10] Wood, *A Commentary On Daniel*, pp. 285-86.

[11] Walvoord, *Daniel*, p. 261.

[12] Wood, *A Commentary On Daniel*, p. 287.

[13] Walvoord, *Daniel*, p. 261.

[14] Young, *The Prophecy Of Daniel*, p. 238.

[15] H. C. Leupold, *Exposition Of Daniel* (Grand Rapids: Baker Book House, 1949), p. 486.

[16] Walvoord, *Daniel*, p. 261.

[17] Wood, *A Commentary On Daniel*, p. 288.

[18] *Ibid.*

[19] *Ibid.*, pp. 288-89.

[20] *Ibid.*, p. 289.

[21] *Ibid.*, p. 290.

[22] Leupold, *Exposition Of Daniel*, p. 489.

[23] *Ibid.*

[24] Wood, *A Commentary On Daniel,* p. 291.

[25] Young, *The Prophecy Of Daniel*, p. 240.

[26] Wood, *A Commentary On Daniel*, pp. 292-93.

[27] Walvoord, *Daniel,* p. 263.

[28] Wood, *A Commentary On Daniel*, pp. 293-94.

[29] Walvoord, *Daniel*, p. 264.

[30] Wood, *A Commentary On Daniel*, p. 294.

[31] Will Durant, *The Life Of Greece* (New York: Simon and Schuster, 1939), p. 574.

[32] Walvoord, *Daniel*, pp. 264-65.

[33] *Ibid.*, p. 265.

[34] Wood, *A Commentary On Daniel*, p. 295.

[35] Young, *The Prophecy Of Daniel*, p. 242.

[36] *Ibid.*

[37] Wood, *A Commentary On Daniel*, pp. 297-99.

[38] Young, *The Prophecy Of Daniel*, p. 243.
[39] Wood, *A Commentary On Daniel*, pp. 300-301.
[40] *Ibid.*, p. 302.
[41] Karl Feyerabend, *Langenscheidt Pocket Hebrew Dictionary* (New York: McGraw-Hill Book Company, 1969), p. 240.
[42] Walvoord, *Daniel*, pp. 270-73.
[43] *Ibid.*, p. 271.
[44] Wood, *A Commentary On Daniel*, p. 304.
[45] *Ibid.*, p. 305.
[46] Young, *The Prophecy Of Daniel*, p. 248.
[47] *Ibid.*, p. 249.
[48] Feyerabend, *Langenscheidt Pocket Hebrew Dictionary*, p. 33.
[49] Wood, *A Commentary On Daniel*, p. 313.
[50] Young, *The Prophecy Of Daniel*, p. 255.
[51] Wood, *A Commentary On Daniel*, p. 319.
[52] Walvoord, *Daniel*, p. 290.

## Chapter 12:4-13

[1] Edward J. Young, *The Prophecy Of Daniel* (Grand Rapids: Wm. B. Eerdmans Publishing Company, 1970), p. 257.
[2] *Ibid.*
[3] Leon Wood, *A Commentary On Daniel* (Grand Rapids: Zondervan Publishing House, 1973), p. 321.
[4] Young, *The Prophecy Of Daniel*, p. 258.
[5] Wood, *A Commentary On Daniel*, p. 323.
[6] *Ibid.*
[7] *Ibid.*, p. 325.
[8] Young, *The Prophecy Of Daniel*, p. 260.
[9] Wood, *A Commentary On Daniel*, p. 325.
[10] *Ibid.*
[11] *Ibid.*, pp. 326-27.
[12] *Ibid.*, p. 328.
[13] *Ibid.*
[14] *Ibid.*
[15] *Ibid.*
[16] Young, *The Prophecy Of Daniel*, p. 264.
[17] Wood, *A Commentary On Daniel*, p. 329.
[18] *Ibid.*
[19] *Ibid.*

# SELECTED BIBLIOGRAPHY

## BOOKS

Anderson, Sir Robert. *The Coming Prince.* Grand Rapids: Kregel Publications, 1954.

Barnes, Albert. *Notes On The Book Of Daniel.* London: George Routledge & Co., 1853.

Boutflower, Charles. *In And Around The Book Of Daniel.* Grand Rapids: Zondervan Publishing House, 1963.

Caldecott, W. Shaw. *Herod's Temple.* London: Charles H. Kelly, n.d.

Cook, S. A., Adcock, F. E. and Charlesworth, M. P. *The Augustan Empire, 44 B.C. - 70 A.D.,* Vol. X: *The Cambridge Ancient History.* Cambridge: The University Press, 1963.

Durant, Will. *Our Oriental Heritage.* New York: Simon and Schuster, 1954.

———. *The Life Of Greece.* New York: Simon and Schuster, 1939.

Feyerabend, Karl. *Langenscheidt Pocket Hebrew Dictionary.* New York: McGraw-Hill Book Company, 1969.

Finegan, Jack. *Handbook Of Biblical Chronology.* Princeton: Princeton University Press, 1964.

Keil, C. F. *Biblical Commentary On The Book Of Daniel.* Grand Rapids: Wm. B. Eerdmans Publishing Company, 1959.

Leupold, H. C. *Exposition Of Daniel.* Grand Rapids: Baker Book House, 1949.

Mc Clain, Alva J. *Daniel's Prophecy Of The 70 Weeks.* Grand Rapids, Zondervan Publishing House, 1978.

Montgomery, James A. *The Book Of Daniel.* New York: Charles Scribner's Sons, 1927.

Olmstead, A. T. *History Of The Persian Empire.* Chicago: The University of Chicago Press, 1959.

Payne, J. Barton. *The Theology Of The Older Testament.* Grand Rapids: Zondervan Publishing House, 1962.

Ramsay, W. M. *Luke The Physician.* New York: A. C. Armstrong and Son, 1908.

Schultz, Samuel J. *The Old Testament Speaks.* New York: Harper & Brothers, Publishers, 1960.

Van Sickle, C. E. *A Political And Cultural History Of The Ancient World.*

2 vols. Chicago: Houghton Mifflin Company, 1947.

Velikovsky, Immanuel. *Worlds In Collision.* New York: Dell Publishing Co., Inc., 1965.

Walvoord, John F. *Daniel.* Chicago: Moody Press, 1971.

Whitcomb, John C. *Darius The Mede.* Grand Rapids: Wm. B. Eerdmans Publishing Company, 1959.

Wood, Leon. *A Commentary On Daniel.* Grand Rapids: Zondervan Publishing House, 1973.

Young, Edward J. *The Prophecy Of Daniel.* Grand Rapids: Wm. B. Eerdmans Publishing Company, 1970.

## ENCYCLOPEDIA ARTICLES

Couderc, Paul. "Calendar — Year." *The Encyclopedia Americana.* 1969. Vol. V.

Ogg, G. "Chronology Of The New Testament." *The New Bible Dictionary.* 1962.

Pinches, T. G. "Chaldea, Chaldeans." *The International Standard Bible Encyclopedia.* 1957. Vol. I.

## JOURNAL ARTICLE

Showers, Renald E. "New Testament Chronology And The Decree Of Daniel 9." *Grace Journal,* XI (Winter, 1970), 30-39.

## UNPUBLISHED MATERIAL

Whitcomb, John C. Unpublished class notes. Grace Theological Seminary, Winona Lake, Indiana, 1969.

# SUBJECT INDEX

*NOTE: Italic* numbers in this Index refer to illustrations, and **boldface** numbers to diagrams.

# H

# N

# T

# U

# SCRIPTURE INDEX

*NOTE: Italic* numbers in this Index refer to pages on which the verses listed are cited.

216

# More Books by
## Renald E. Showers

**MARANATHA: OUR LORD, COME!**
*A Definitive Study of the Rapture of the Church*
This in-depth study addresses such issues as the Day of the Lord, its relationship to the Time of Jacob's Trouble and the Great Tribulation, the 70 Weeks of Daniel, and much more. Learn why the timing of the Rapture has practical implications for daily living and ministry.
ISBN 0-915540-22-3, #B55P

**THERE REALLY IS A DIFFERENCE!**
*A Comparison of Covenant and Dispensational Theology*
Learn how theological differences affect such issues as God's ultimate purpose for history, God's program for Israel, the church, and the Christian's relationship to the Mosaic Law and grace. This excellent book also explores the differences between the premillennial, amillennial, and postmillennial views of the Kingdom of God and presents an apology for the dispensational-premillennial system of theology.
ISBN 0-915540-50-9, #B36

220

## THOSE INVISIBLE SPIRITS CALLED ANGELS
Much is said about angels these days. But how much of it is correct? This excellent, easy-to-read volume teaches what the Bible says about angels—who they are, what they do, and how they minister to us.
ISBN 0-915540-24-X, #B66

## TWO MILLENNIA OF CHURCH HISTORY
This comprehensive, easy-to-understand, and beautifully illustrated 24-page booklet puts 2,000 years of church history at your fingertips. An exceptional resource, it will enable you to trace the development of first-century Orthodoxy, Romanism, the Reformation, liberal theology, the great spiritual awakenings, and much, much more.
ISBN 0-915540-67-3, #B82

## THE FOUNDATIONS OF FAITH
### Volume 1
This is a compiliation of Dr. Showers' in-depth studies in systematic theology. *The Revealed and Personal Word of God* is the first in the series and covers bibliology and Chrisology—the doctrines of the Bible and the Messiah. This hardback, fully indexed volume is a must for any serious student of God's Word.
ISBN 0-915540-77-0, #B89